THE MAGNIFICENT
MONTMORENCY

PLATE I

HENRY DVC DE MONTMORENÇY ET D'AM-
VILLE PAIR, ET MARESCHAL DE FRANCE,
Et Lieutenant gñal pour le ROY *en Languedoc.*

THE MAGNIFICENT MONTMORENCY

THE LIFE AND DEATH OF
HENRI DUC DE MONTMORENCY
1595–1632

BY
CYRIL HUGHES HARTMANN
M.A., B.Litt., Author of ' The Vagabond Duchess'.
' The Story of the Roads', etc.

LONDON
GEORGE ROUTLEDGE & SONS, LTD.
NEW YORK: E. P. DUTTON & CO.
1928

PRINTED IN GREAT BRITAIN BY PURNELL AND SONS
PAULTON (SOMERSET) AND LONDON

TO
MY WIFE

CONTENTS

CHAPTER I

CHAPTER II

CHAPTER III

CHAPTER IV

CHAPTER V

CHAPTER VI

CHAPTER VII

CHAPTER VIII

CHAPTER XI

EPILOGUE

LIST OF ILLUSTRATIONS

PREFACE

My attention was first directed to Montmorency some two years ago, when a contemporary manuscript description of his trial and execution came into my possession. Before that time I had known little of him beyond the fact that he was a great nobleman executed for opposition to Richelieu and rebellion against Louis XIII. The tragic story unfolded in this document so appealed to me that I was impelled, as soon as I had leisure, to look further into his career. I found that there was no modern full-length biography of the Duke himself even in French, though his wife, owing to the holiness of her life, had been the subject of several monographs. Marie Félice de Montmorency at first struck me as being so aggressively virtuous that I must confess that I started somewhat prejudiced against her. But I was soon forced to accord her my respectful homage; she seems, when conscious, to have been an admirable wife to Montmorency. I have not thought fit to pursue her career after her husband's death; for such as have the curiosity to do so there exist already four biographies of varying interest. I must acknowledge my debt to these as well as to several other modern works, though I have endeavoured to found my account of the Duke's career upon contemporary works as far as possible. The authorities from which my narrative has been derived are fully discussed in the Bibliographical Appendix.

In regard to the illustrations: I have selected the Lasne engraving of Montmorency as being better than that by Mellan prefixed to Du Cros' *Life*. I have not been able to find any portrait of the Duchess showing her as she appeared during her husband's lifetime, and have therefore been obliged to fall back on Van Schuppen's engraving of her in the habit of her order. The remainder of the illustrations have been chosen less for their artistic merit, which, in the case of the Moncornet engravings at least, is but meagre, than for their value as *illustrations* to the book in the literal sense of the term. There are, for instance, many portraits of Cardinal Richelieu infinitely better than the one reproduced here ; but none could be more appropriate to the story than this picture of the man who supplanted the Grand Admiral of France.

CYRIL HUGHES HARTMANN.

CHAPTER I

Birth of Montmorency—His lineage—The Constable
Anne—Henri I de Montmorency—His career—His love
for Mary Stuart—Enmity of Catherine de Medici and
Henri III towards him—He espouses the cause of
Henri of Navarre—Made Constable by Henri IV—His
illiteracy—His friendship with Henry IV—His love-
affairs—His marriages—Death of his second wife,
Louise de Budos—Henri II de Montmorency—His
baptism—The Constable's third marriage—Description
of Montmorency—His squint—The King's affection for
him—His strict upbringing—His generosity—The King
projects marrying him to one of his natural daughters
—The Constable does not approve the royal choice—
He secretly arranges to marry his son to a Breton heiress
—Montmorency's flight into Brittany with his uncle
—The King tries to have the fugitives arrested—The
marriage takes place—Montmorency and his bride
attend the wedding of Charlotte de Condé—The King
causes the marriage to be annulled—Montmorency
affianced to Mademoiselle de Vendôme—Assassination
of Henri IV—Montmorency's horsemanship—The tournament in the Place Royale—Montmorency as the
Perseus of France—Description of his cavalcade—The
procession to the Louvre.

At half-past eight in the evening on the 30th
of April, 1595, a son and heir was born at his
Château of Chantilly to the Constable Henri de
Montmorency, the head of one of the most illustrious families in all France. The Montmorencys
not only possessed certain privileges above all the

rest of the nobility, but also claimed the same precedence as those who held the rank of prince. Their boasts were indeed proud, as witness this extract from an ancient heraldic work: '*Montmorency premier Chrestien que Roy en France: premier Seigneur de Mont-morency que Roy en France: premier Baron de France: sur son tymbre port un Paon qui fait la roue; son cry est "Dieu ayde au premier Chrestien"; son mot est "Απλανως, c'est à dire "Sans Tache".*'[1] The ancient barony of Montmorency was held directly from the Crown, a golden falcon being due on each succession, but the Duchy, although it took precedence over all others in France, was of comparatively recent date, having been created in 1551 by King Henri II in favour of the Constable Anne de Montmorency and his heirs male.

The Constable Anne was an illustrious warrior throughout his long life—he served under five kings of France—and eventually met a soldier's death from wounds received at the siege of St. Denis in 1567. When he was carried dying from the field of battle to his house in Paris, those with him exhorted him to bear his wounds with patience. The Constable proudly answered them: "A man who has known how to live for seventy-five years ought to know how to die in a quarter of an hour."[2]

[1] Quoted by Du Chesne.   [2] Rénée, 242.

Anne de Montmorency was succeeded by his son, François, who, dying in 1579 predeceased by his only child, was followed in his honours by his younger brother, Henri. Henri I, Duc de Montmorency, was renowned for his bravery. Even during the lifetime of his father he had gained great military reputation under the cadet family title of Baron de Damville. He had particularly distinguished himself at the battle of Dreux in 1562 when at the head of the cavalry he had broken the ranks of the Swiss Guards no less than seven times. Nothing could daunt him, although his father had been taken prisoner and he had seen his younger brother, Gabriel, Baron de Montbéron, killed before his very eyes. When all seemed lost and he himself was wounded and unhorsed, he procured a horse from a trooper in his company and, rallying his men, charged the victorious Condé and changed the tide of battle, taking Condé himself prisoner. While still a young man he was already a Marshal of France and Governor of Languedoc.

The most romantic episode in his romantic career was his love for Mary Stuart, then the wife of King François II. His devotion for her was as unconcealed as it was passionate and he openly wore her colours at the tournaments. It is said that she returned his love and would indeed have married him when she became a widow, had not the match been successfully opposed by her relatives, the Guises, hereditary enemies of the house of Montmorency.

Although the Montmorencys were Catholics, Damville had for some reason incurred the enmity of Catherine de Medici, who endeavoured to secure the assassination of his whole family during the massacre of St. Bartholomew. Fortunately Damville was warned and managed to escape and take refuge in Languedoc. The Queen's hatred appears to have been inherited by her son, Henri III. When he returned from Poland to become King of France in 1574 he affected friendship towards Damville, sending him a safe-conduct and requesting him to come and meet him. Damville unsuspectingly obeyed the summons only to find that a treacherous attempt was to be made to arrest him. Once again he was fortunate enough to be warned so that he could escape in time, but he roundly swore that in future all he would see of the King would be portraits of him.[1]

This last bitter experience had sufficed to disgust him for ever with the house of Valois, and he determined to throw in his lot with the Protestant party headed by Henri of Navarre, who, like himself, had fled from Court for safety. In view of his conduct Henri III decided to dispossess him of his government of Languedoc and to grant

---

[1] Rénée, 13.

it to his favourite, Joyeuse. But Damville did not intend to give it up without a fight and met Joyeuse and slew him at the battle of Coutras. Henceforth his influence was paramount in the south of France. He remained steadfast in the interests of Henri of Navarre, although he was approached with the most advantageous offers both by the Guises and by Philip II of Spain. Henri III actually had the effrontery to appeal to him for help when he was expelled from Paris, but Damville naturally enough would have nothing further to do with him. On the death of Henri III he was instrumental in persuading the Catholic nobility of the south to recognise the King of Navarre's claim to the throne. Henri of Navarre did not prove ungrateful. As soon as he was firmly seated on the throne as Henri IV he fitly rewarded the faithful services of Damville, now through his brother's death Duc de Montmorency, by sending him the sword of Constable.

The new Constable, who was the sixth Montmorency[1] to hold that exalted office, was first and foremost a man of war. Although he possessed much natural astuteness, he was almost entirely devoid of culture, and, in the words of his son's biographer, Du Cros, 'had read no book save that

[1] The others were Alberic, Thibault, Mathieu I, Mathieu II, and Anne.

of the world.' Both Cardinal Richelieu and Tallemant des Réaux enlarge upon his illiteracy, and in truth he seems to have been scarcely able to read, while his handwriting was as painful for him to execute as it was for others to decipher. Henri IV was wont to rally him on the deficiencies in his education. On one occasion he drily remarked: "With this friend of mine who can neither read nor write, and my Chancellor, who knows no Latin, there is nothing that I could not undertake."[1]

Henri IV and the Constable de Montmorency remained always the most intimate of friends and the King lost no occasion of doing him honour. When he created the dukedom of Beaufort for César de Vendôme, his son by Gabrielle d'Estrées, and desired to give it precedence over all the other dukedoms of France, he expressly excepted that of Montmorency.[2]

Between the King and the Constable there was a friendly rivalry as to who could indulge in the greater number of amorous adventures. The Constable's love-intrigues seem to have been as numerous as they were promiscuous. He has indeed been accused of not having shown too strict a regard for the laws of affinity. Tallemant des Réaux says that he doubts if he went so far in this respect as people said, but that he cer-

[1] Rénée, 15.   [2] Rénée, 229.

tainly showed no scruples as regards his aunts, sisters, cousins, or nieces.

In addition to his countless amours the Constable was married three times. By his first wife, Antoinette de la Marck, daughter of the Duc de Bouillon, he had two sons, both of whom died young, and two daughters, Charlotte and Marguerite, the elder of whom later married the Duc d'Angoulême and the younger the Duc de Ventadour. The Constable's first wife died in 1591, and two years later he married a young widow, Louise de Budos, daughter of the Vicomte de Portes and widow of Jacques de Grammont, Seigneur de Vachères. The young woman, although of noble birth, was scarcely possessed of the exalted rank expected in the wife of the Constable of France, so that when she died of apoplexy at an early age it was whispered that she had made a solemn compact with the devil to bring about the alliance.[1] A detailed legend to this effect was for long handed down in the Condé family. On her death in 1598 at the early age of twenty-three and at the zenith of her beauty she left her husband with two small children, Charlotte Marguerite, born in 1594, and a son, Henri, born a year later.

The boy was of the nineteenth generation in direct male descent from Bouchard, who flourished in the reign of King Lothaire and may properly

[1] Tallemant des Réaux,

be regarded as the founder of the house of Montmorency, since before his time the history of the
family is somewhat apocryphal.[1] The Constable's
heir was not baptised until the 5th of March, 1597,
when he was two years old. The christening
ceremony was performed by the papal legate;
the child was held by the King himself who stood
godfather and gave the boy his own name; and
the royal mistress, Gabrielle d'Estrées, graced the
occasion with her presence. In this same year
the King declared his godson heir to the government of Languedoc and two years later appointed
him Governor of Narbonne.

In 1601 the Constable obtained a papal
dispensation to marry his second wife's aunt,
Laurence de Clermont Montoison, widow of Jean,
Comte de Dizimieu. This marriage caused general
astonishment, since the lady was neither young
nor beautiful; some, indeed, went so far as to say
that he married her simply because she was ready
to hand,[2] and there may be some truth in this,
for she appears to have taken charge of his
children after her niece's death. Being childless
herself she adored the children, and they appear
to have returned her affection. But the Constable himself speedily grew tired of her and after
three months of married life relegated her to
banishment in the provinces.

[1] Du Cros, 3.   [2] Tallemant des Réaux.

The young Henri, who was brought up chiefly at his father's castles of Chantilly and Merlou, grew up into a most handsome lad. He was tall and straight with a graceful figure, curling golden hair, and beautiful features. His sole defect was the slight squint which was characteristic of his family, but which contemporary observers declare was rather attractive than otherwise. The very fact that he himself was devoid of learning made the Constable doubly anxious that his son should have every advantage in this respect, but he did not disguise his pleasure when the boy showed an early preference for martial exercises. He was a great favourite with the King, who spoilt him outrageously, to the Constable's mingled pride and disgust. Henri IV enjoyed nothing better than getting the little boy to talk and endeavouring to give him his first lessons in statesmanship. It is related that one day he asked him what he thought was the greatest quality a monarch could possess. Without hesitation young Montmorency answered that it was clemency. Somewhat surprised, the King enquired why he had fixed upon clemency rather than upon courage or liberality, both of which were surely necessary in a king. The boy replied that he had done so because to kings alone in this world belonged the power of punishment or pardon.[1] The little boy also had

[1] Pitaval, 8.

an admirer in Queen Marguerite de Valois, who once said that if it had pleased God to give her a son she would have asked nothing better than that he should have resembled little Henri de Montmorency.[1] On one occasion the King remarked to his minister, Villeroy: "Look at my son Montmorency, how handsome he is! If ever the house of Bourbon should fail, there is no family in Europe which would merit the Crown of France so much as his, whose great men have always sustained its glory and even increased it at the price of their blood."[2]

In order to counteract the King's excessive indulgence the Constable determined to have the boy brought up strictly, and ordered his governor, Du Travet, to subject him to thorough discipline in every particular.[3] Nothing, however, could suppress the extravagant generosity that was to be one of his most distinguishing characteristics throughout his life. His father gave the governor strict orders that this disposition in him was to be severely curbed, but the boy could not be prevented from finding outlets for his generosity. The tale is told that when he was still a child he helped one of his gentlemen who was hard pressed for money by giving him one of his most valuable pieces of jewelry and pretending that he had lost it.[4]

[1] Desormeaux, 191.   [3] Baillon, 17.
[2] Ibid.   [4] Du Cros, 9; Desormeaux, 190.

It was Henri IV's cherished project to marry this handsome godson of his to one of his own natural daughters; but though the Constable welcomed the idea in principle, the King and he found themselves unable to agree as to which daughter it should be. The Constable wished for Mademoiselle de Vendôme,[1] but the King had already promised her to the house of Longueville and offered Mademoiselle de Verneuil[2] instead. This alliance the Constable refused, to the intense annoyance of the King, who was so angry that he ordered him to retire in disgrace to his castle of Chantilly, while he kept the boy at Court with him.[3] But the Constable did not relish being treated in so high-handed a manner, and resolved to spite the King by secretly arranging for his son's marriage to a young Breton heiress of immense fortune and illustrious lineage, Jeanne de Scépeaux de Chemillé, Duchesse de Beaupréau. The adventurous boy was easily persuaded to join in a project which promised to afford much excitement and amusement, and he managed to escape from the Louvre and ride away into Brittany with his uncle, the Baron de Damville,

[1] Catherine Henriette, daughter of Gabrielle d'Estrées. In 1619 she married Charles de Lorraine, Duc d'Elbeuf. She died in 1663.

[2] Gabrielle Angélique, daughter of Henriette de Balzac d'Entragues. In 1622 she married Bernard de Nogaret, Duc d'Epernon. She died in 1627.

[3] Desormeaux, 193.

who was in the plot.[1] The Constable had
arranged that they were to proceed to one of
his country-houses, Gonor, near to the place
where the heiress and her mother were to await
them.

When the King heard what had happened he
was furious and at once had the fugitives pursued. A message was sent to Du Plessis Mornay,
Governor of Saumur, to arrest them. As soon
as he heard of their arrival the Governor hastened
to wait on Damville, who received him in a most
friendly manner and invited him to dine with
him and his nephew. The Governor declined, but,
thinking that it would hardly be polite to arrest
distinguished noblemen just before dinner, he
placed sentinels outside the inn and resolved to
return and execute his orders a little later. But
his visit had aroused Damville's suspicions and
instead of proceeding to dinner he and Montmorency slipped out to the stables, saddled their
horses, and hastily made their escape from the
town. A few leagues further on they were in
safety, for they fell in with a troop of fifty gentlemen whom the Constable had arranged to be
in readiness to escort them. The King had considered it possible that they might succeed in

---

[1] Charles de Montmorency, a younger brother of the Constable.
He had first born the title of Seigneur de Méru, but assumed that of
Baron de Damville when Henri became Duc de Montmorency. He
was created Duc de Damville in 1610, the year after these events.

evading the Governor's vigilance and had
endeavoured to add another string to his bow
by ordering the Duc de Soubise with two companies of light horse to go and kidnap the bride.
But this expedient also failed, for when Soubise
arrived he found that the wedding had already
taken place.[1]

That the marriage was officially recognized at
Court is proved by the list of guests who attended
the wedding of the Constable's daughter, Charlotte
Marguerite de Montmorency, to the Prince de
Condé on the 2nd of March, 1609. Among them
were 'Henry de Montmorency, Governor for the
King in Languedoc, her only brother, and Dame
Jeanne d'Espeaux, duchesse de Beaupréau, wife
of the said seigneur de Montmorency.'[2] But
although the marriage was an accomplished fact
and it was said that it had actually been consummated, Henri IV did not allow so trifling an
obstacle to deter him from his views regarding
young Montmorency's future. He adopted the
simple plan of having the marriage annulled on
the ground that Henri de Montmorency was not
yet nubile. As he was then fourteen or fifteen
years old and particularly robust and well-grown
for his age the pretext caused much ribald amusement at Court. The ceremony of annulment was
carried out unostentatiously at the Jesuits' church

[1] Desormeaux, 193–4; Pitaval, 10–11.   [2] Aumale, II, 445,

in Paris, and it seems that the Constable himself
was a party to the arrangement, since he had
discovered that the alliance was not so advantageous as he had hoped and believed.[1] The
heiress, who was seven years older than her bridegroom, cannot have been seriously disturbed at
being deprived of so very youthful a husband,
and not many months had passed before she
consoled herself with a marriage to the Duc de
Retz.[2]

The incident had sufficed to convince the King
that the Constable was not to be trifled with,
and so he persuaded the Longueville family to
renounce their claim to the hand of Mademoiselle
de Vendôme and forthwith affianced her to Henri
de Montmorency. Matters stood thus when on
May the 14th, 1610, the King was assassinated;
but the marriage never took place, for the widowed
queen, Marie de Medici, had very different ideas
as to the future of this son and heir of one of the
most illustrious houses in France, though the time
was not yet ripe to put her project into execution. The bride she destined for him was not yet
ten years old. Henri de Montmorency himself
was only fifteen and scarcely too old to be a com-
panion to her own small son, the new King of

---

[1] Pitaval, 12.
[2] Rénée, 8. Du Cros is tactfully evasive in his allusions to this
escapade. He simply remarks that the Chemillé marriage did not
meet with the King's approval.

France. As a matter of fact he was one of the first in the kingdom to swear allegiance to him after his father's death, since he happened to be out driving with him in his carriage at the time of the assassination and returned to the Louvre with him.[1]

Henri de Montmorency at the age of seventeen or eighteen had certainly become one of the most brilliantly attractive young men at the Court of France. His good looks, his charm, his generosity, and his courage won the hearts of both men and women. He shone particularly in manly exercises. He was one of the best horsemen in the land, having inherited his love of horseflesh from his father, who possessed a veritable passion for horses. 'As soon as a horse became his,' says Tallemant des Réaux, 'it never again changed masters, and if it had only three legs they would still care for it in a hospital at Chantilly.' Young Montmorency himself had been able to master the most restive steed at an age when he could scarcely have been expected to straddle it.[2] He had learnt to ride the great horse at Chantilly in the company of other young men of his age, including a young English nobleman, Lord Herbert of Cherbury. Nothing delighted Montmorency more than to show off his magnificent horsemanship in mock-fights and tournaments.

[1] Du Cros, 10.   [2] Du Cros, 7.

He distinguished himself particularly at the great tournament held in the Place Royale on the 5th, 6th, and 7th of April, 1612, to celebrate the betrothal of the young king, Louis XIII.

The tournament of the 17th century was no less resplendent but much less dangerous than the jousts of medieval times when armed knights rode against each other. The knights on this occasion proved their skill by tilting at the quintain on the first two days and riding at the ring on the third. The King, the Queen-Regent, Queen Marguerite de Valois, and the Princesses attended in state, and the Constable sat with the Marshals of France, Bouillon, Brissac, Bois-Dauphin, and Lesdiguières as judges of the tournament. Some eighty thousand people were accommodated in stands around the square in which was erected an elaborate and fantastic edifice called the Palace of Happiness. A galaxy of young noblemen, including the Duc de Guise, the Duc de Nevers, the Prince de Joinville, and Bassompierre were supposed to be the denizens of this palace, and, under the name of the Knights of Glory, challenged all comers to test their prowess in the lists against them. The Prince de Conti, the Duc de Vendôme, Montmorency, and other great noblemen formed ten companies of assailants. The processions of these various companies with their heralds, attendants, allegorical figures, and

decorated triumphal cars vied one with another
in their gorgeousness, and not the least magnificent
was that of Montmorency who represented the
Perseus of France.[1]

The order of Montmorency's procession was as
follows:—

A mounted aide-de-camp magnificently ap-
parelled.

Eight mounted trumpeters habited as Zephyrs
in carnation-coloured satin and green velvet with
wings fastened to their backs. They were
crowned with garlands of flowers. The trappings
of their horses were of green velvet heavily embroidered with silver.

Twelve slaves representing the nations con-
quered by Perseus. They walked two by two
dressed as Tartars, Indians, and Chinese, wearing
golden chains and with their garments covered
with gold and silver embroidery and precious
stones. Each led a Spanish horse caparisoned in
the style of the country he represented.

Twelve footmen in gold-embroidered liveries of
green and carnation-colour.

Ten mounted pages in carnation-coloured velvet
and green satin embroidered with gold. Each
carried a lance adorned with a pennant of carnation-
coloured taffeta bearing Montmorency's cipher.

---

[1] *Mercure François*, 1612, II, pp. 331–357; Rénée, 11–12;
Desormeaux, 196–7.

c

Four squires in costumes of ancient style made of cloth of gold with sleeves of carnation-colour also embroidered with gold. Their helmets were covered with floating plumes of carnation-colour from the midst of which rose enormous aigrettes. On their left arms they bore shields with the arms of Montmorency. They were mounted on superb Spanish horses.

Montmorency de Bouteville's squire in dove-coloured satin embroidered with silver.

Four footmen similarly attired.

Louis de Montmorency de Bouteville, Vice-Admiral of France, who was acting on this occasion as maréchal-de-camp to his cousin. He rode a superb horse and was splendidly attired in amaranth velvet covered with golden embroidery. His hat surmounted with heron's plumes was adorned with a band of precious stones and a diamond brooch.

A herald in Turkish costume of satin embroidered with gold and silver. He carried a golden scimitar studded with pearls and diamonds and a scutcheon with the Montmorency arms.

Montmorency's parade-horse, magnificently harnessed, led by two Persian slaves with gold collars round their necks.

Montmorency's charger led by two men representing Argus in dresses covered with eyes.

A slave in cloth of gold preceding the triumphal car drawn by six gold-antlered stags caparisoned in carnation-coloured satin embroidered with gold. The car, which was blazing with gold, was covered with trophies of arms and bronze figures of captives. The coachman was habited as Saturn with his scythe. Behind him stood golden figures representing the three Graces, and above them the goddess of Peace dressed in white satin embroidered with silver, a garland of flowers about her head and an olive-branch in her hand. She was seated upon a drum and beneath her feet lay the broken arms of war. Behind her again were two golden harpies bearing on their heads gilded vases which supported two steps covered with a gold-embroidered carpet leading to a golden throne on which sat Henri de Montmorency himself attired as Perseus in a gold cuirass covered with pearls. The sleeves were of carnation-coloured satin embroidered with pearls and gold. Beneath his feet lay a representation of the bleeding carcase of the Gorgon Medusa, whose head was painted on the shield he carried on his left arm. On either side of him stood a beautiful deity, the one representing France, the other Spain, with crowns and sceptres studded with jewels of inestimable value. The whole car was surmounted by a pavilion of cloth of gold in which stood a girl in white satin representing Fame.

Behind the car followed six captive gods in chains: Mars, Neptune, Vulcan, Pluto, Mercury, and Hercules, each appropriately costumed.

Pegasus, the winged horse of Perseus, led by two slaves.

A towering silver rock advancing amidst a rough sea, and behind it a vast silver-scaled sea-monster in chains. Transfixed by Perseus' dart it gushed forth blood and vainly struggled in the waves.

Last of all twelve hautboy-players, attired in green satin as sylvan deities with flowing locks and head-dresses of oak-leaves and golden acorns.

In order that the people who could not find room in the Place Royale might have an opportunity of seeing the show the Queen-Regent arranged that those who had taken part in the tournament should go in procession to the Louvre on the evening of the third and last day of the festivities. The streets were decorated and coloured lanterns were placed in every window. So long was the procession that it took two hours to pass and it was midnight before the tail of it had reached the Louvre.

CHAPTER II

The Constable retires to Languedoc—Montmorency
becomes Admiral of France and Duc de Montmorency
—Marie de Medici projects his marriage—Marie Félice
des Ursins—Her childhood—Her leanings towards a
religious life—She consents to marry Montmorency—
The contract signed in Rome and Paris—The proxy
marriage—The bride's grief at parting from her family
—The Constable meets her at Avignon—Montmorency's
disinclination for the marriage—His desire to marry
another frustrated—His magnificent appearance at the
Louvre—Marie Félice falls in love at first sight—Louis
XIII introduces husband and wife—Marie Félice's
'merits and perfections'—Her lack of beauty—Her
father snubs a too flattering painter—The wedding—
Montmorency quarrels with the Duc de Retz—He con-
ceals the matter from his wife—The duel—The adver-
saries reconciled—Marie Félice attributes Montmorency's
safety to a holy image she had given him—Death of
the Constable—Montmorency goes to Languedoc—
Marie Félice left behind—The Queen's affection for her
—She avoids politics—Attempts by La Galigai and
others to involve her in intrigues—She secures the
release of Angoulême—A retired life—Marie Félice
learns French—Her letters to her husband intercepted
by the princesses—The Queen returns them unread—
The Duchess's faithfulness to her husband—Story of
the gloves—She avoids functions at Court—The King's
marriage at Bordeaux—Unexpected appearance of
Montmorency—The journey back to Paris—The Duchess
ill at Poitiers—The Montmorencys at Chantilly—
Arrest of the Prince de Condé—Civil War—Murder of
the Maréchal d'Ancre—Montmorency's reception of

the news—Rise of Luynes—Montmorency resolves to
remain in Languedoc.

In June, 1612, the aged Constable took his final
leave of the Court and went away to Languedoc
with the intention of ending his days there in the
peace of a country life.[1] His retirement meant
that his son came into greater prominence. He had
already soon after his birth been declared heir to
the government of Languedoc and when he was
still a mere boy his father had taken him to Montpellier to proclaim him formally. A week's festivities were held in his honour, and two thousand
strangers from all parts of the province flocked
into the town to acclaim him.[2] A month after
his father's retirement, when he was still only
seventeen, he was made Admiral of France,
Guienne, and Gascony in succession to his uncle,
the Duc de Damville, whose duchy he also inherited by special remainder. A year later his
father resigned the duchy of Montmorency to him
and he was created a peer of France.

About this time his marriage took place. Just
as Henri IV had always had a particular affection
for his godson Henri de Montmorency, so his queen,
Marie de Medici, had taken under her special pro-
tection her god-daughter Marie Félice Orsini,
daughter of Virginio Orsini, Duca di Bracciano,

---

[1] Bassompierre, I, 309.
[2] Du Cros, 8; Aigrefeuille, 346; Desormeaux, 192.

and of Fulvia Peretti, a great-niece of Pope
Sixtus V.[1] The Orsinis, or, as the French called
them, the Des Ursins, were a very ancient and
illustrious family which had produced countless
generals and cardinals, besides two popes and
several saints.[2] The Duca di Bracciano himself
was General of the Galleys of Tuscany and had
served with distinction against the Turks and the
corsairs of the Mediterranean. Marie Félice was
one of ten children and the third and youngest
daughter. She was born in Rome on November
the 11th, 1600, about a month after Marie de
Medici had left for France to marry Henri IV.[3]
Before her departure the future Queen of France
had promised to be godmother to the expected
child, and when it proved to be a girl she gave
her her own name. At the Court of France
malicious tongues whispered that the Queen's
predilection for Marie Félice was inspired by
sentimental recollections of her father who
was supposed to have been a former lover of
hers.

Through one of her grandmothers, Elizabeth de
Medici, Marie Félice possessed a certain kinship to
that illustrious house, and at the request of the
Grand Duchess of Tuscany she and her sisters

[1] Rénée, 324
[2] The Duchess's biographer, Cotolendi, asserts that the saints
numbered no less than twenty-two.
[3] Baillon, 5.

were sent to Florence to be brought up with her
own family.[1] At the end of a year the Grand
Duchess placed Marie Félice in a Benedictine
convent in the same city in order to complete her
education. The intelligent child possessed a
natural inclination for learning and early mas-
tered the intricacies of Latin and Greek. But she
showed a special disposition towards a religious
life and it soon became her ambition to take the
veil, a plan which did not commend itself to Marie
de Medici, who had made up her mind to bring
her to France by marrying her to some member of
the French nobility.

No one more suitable could possibly have been
found than young Henri de Montmorency, who,
besides possessing the necessary rank and riches,
was just of the right age, being five years older
than his prospective bride. The Constable's
consent was obtained without difficulty, especially
as Marie Félice was provided with the ample
dowry of 450,000 livres, of which the Queen herself
furnished 300,000.[2] The Marquis de Traisnel,[3] a
cousin of the Duca de Bracciano, was sent to Rome
to negotiate the marriage. Bracciano welcomed
the prospect of so brilliant an alliance for his
youngest daughter, but, unlike most fathers of his
time, he was unwilling to give his consent without

[1] Cotolendi, 2.   [2] Baillon, 18.
[3] François Jouvenel des Ursins, Marquis de Traisnel or Tresnel

first consulting the wishes of Marie Félice herself. He accordingly journeyed to Florence to discuss the matter with her. Marie Félice was of a tractable disposition, and although her longings were still bent towards a religious life, she consented readily enough to please her family by this marriage. The contract was signed in Rome on August the 10th, 1613, and on November the 25th it received in Paris the additional signatures of the young king, Louis XIII, the Queen-Regent, and the Princes of the Blood Royal.

In December the proxy marriage took place at the Pitti Palace, the Marquis de Traisnel representing the bridegroom. Traisnel and his wife were entrusted with the charge of escorting the young bride to France.

The Orsinis were a very affectionate and united family and the farewells were very painful to them. The bride's father and one of her brothers were so affected that they felt that they could not bear the pains of parting and rode away from Florence without saying good-bye to her. Two of her brothers, however, accompanied her as far as Leghorn.[1] When the final parting came Marie Félice tried hard to be brave, but so difficult was it for her to keep back her tears that in the effort she burst the ribbons of her bodice.[2]

[1] Cotolendi, 2.
[2] Baillon, 21; Rénée, 3. Monlaur (14) says that the whale-bone in her corsets snapped in several places.

Marie Félice's first act after landing at Marseilles was to visit the shrine of St. Mary Magdalen at St. Baume. She then proceeded to Avignon, where she was met by the Constable who professed himself charmed with her and declared that God had spared him only that he might welcome so virtuous a daughter.[1] After two or three days she left for Paris while the Constable went to Languedoc to announce her arrival to his son, who was then paying his first visit as Governor to the province.[2]

Although the Constable gave Henri a glowing account of his bride, it appears that Montmorency himself was inclined to regard the marriage simply as one of convenience, since he was at the time passionately in love with someone else. The object of his affection was a certain lady of Languedoc, who had been married against her will to an old man and had consoled herself with Montmorency. It happened that about this time the elderly husband fell downstairs and killed himself, and Montmorency seems to have been anxious to marry the widow, who was now free. His hopes, however, were frustrated when he was informed that his own marriage had already taken place by proxy and he was no longer at liberty to dispose of his heart and hand.[3]

---

[1] Monlaur, 15.   [2] Du Cros, 13.
[3] Pitaval, 14.

In spite of his reluctance to the marriage Montmorency was not averse to gilding with his usual magnificence the occasion of his first meeting with his bride. He appeared at the Louvre on horseback attended by twenty-four pages and innumerable attendants and escorted by a hundred gentlemen of Languedoc, some of them being of considerable rank and standing in that province. Montmorency easily outshone them all by the brilliance of his appearance, and Marie Félice, who, seated with the King at a window of the Louvre, was watching his arrival, herself avows that she fell in love with him at first sight.[1]

Dismounting in the courtyard, Montmorency proceeded upstairs, where the young king himself advanced to meet him leading Marie Félice by the hand, and introducing them in his own childish way—he was only twelve at the time—"Here is my cousin, the illustrious Italian. Is she good enough for you? Are you pleased with her?" Marie de Medici then came forward and completed the presentation more formally, adding, "I believe that in her person I am giving you the merits and perfections of many others."[2]

Marie Félice's 'merits and perfections' seem in truth to have been mental rather than physical. She had little claim to beauty, though she had a lovely figure which she bore with a regal grace.

[1] Monlaur, 16.   [2] Rénée, 4; Monlaur, 17.

Her greatest attractions were her clear complexion, her expressive black eyes, and a gentle, gracious smile. Mademoiselle de Montpensier says, on the authority of Anne of Austria, that, although she was never really beautiful, she was very agreeable to look upon.[1] At any rate she does not appear to have been brought up with any illusions as to her looks. A certain painter once produced of her a likeness so flattering that her father affected not to recognize it and asked to be shown his daughter's picture. When the painter pointed out his mistake to him Bracciano remarked, "You must either make my daughter resemble the portrait, or the portrait resemble my daughter."[2]

The marriage proper took place with great magnificence in the presence of all the Court at the Louvre, and at the Queen-Regent's pressing invitation the young couple remained with her for some days. During this time the young Duke was involved in a most unfortunate quarrel with the Duc de Retz, husband of the lady whose marriage with Montmorency had formerly been annulled. If the accounts of the origin of the quarrel are true, it is difficult to find any excuse for the bad taste and bad manners displayed by Montmorency. One day at Court some sugar-plums were offered to him. After helping himself

[1] Montpensier, III, 351.   [2] Pitaval, 14.

he handed on the box to Retz saying, *"Prenez, Monsieur, ce ne sera pas la première fois que vous aurez de mes restes."* It is scarcely surprising that Retz took offence at this insulting play upon his name, especially if, as Du Cros asserts, the Duke had made it more than once. Tallemant des Réaux says that the Duke was actually in the habit of referring to Retz as '*le Duc de mon reste*'. If, as he also avers, Montmorency's first marriage was never actually consummated, the poor joke loses even such point of exceedingly doubtful taste as it might ever have possessed. At any rate Retz challenged Montmorency to a duel.

Montmorency said nothing to his wife about the quarrel or the projected duel, but the evening before it was to take place he went into her bed-chamber while she was being undressed and wandered about the room fingering her jewels and the toilet-articles on her dressing-table and laughing and rallying her playfully on the numerous devotional images with which she had surrounded herself. Just before he left, making the excuse that he had work to do, he asked her to give him an Agnus Dei which she always wore about her neck during the night. Marie Félice was delighted by his request and herself fastened it to his sleeve with a ribbon.[1]

[1] Monlaur, 41; Rénée, 10.

As soon as she had fallen asleep Montmorency
slipped out of the Louvre and went to meet his
second, his uncle, the Marquis de Portes. They
passed the night at an inn near the Bastille and
early the next morning went forth to the Porte St.
Antoine where they had arranged to meet Retz.
Accounts of the duel vary.[1] Some say that Montmorency easily disarmed his adversary; others
that he himself was ignominiously disarmed;
others again that he disarmed Retz and in doing
so lost his own sword. The point is of little importance, since neither the skill nor the personal
courage of either of the combatants can be
doubted. At all events the duel was followed by
an immediate reconciliation, and the two erstwhile
enemies returned to Paris and dined together the
best of friends. Marie Félice received the news
of the duel with mingled feelings of horror and
relief. Characteristically she attributed her husband's safe return to the holy image she had
given him and insisted that henceforth he should
always carry it. It is said that he never failed to
do so until the fatal day of the battle of Castelnaudary, when he put on a new suit of clothes and
forgot to give orders to have the reliquary attached
to them.[2] But this appears to be the sort of story
that is only too often manufactured after the event!

[1] See Desormeaux, 201; Pitaval, 19; Monlaur, 14.
[2] Baillon, 28; Monlaur, 42.

The young Montmorencys were not allowed by
fate to remain together for very long. At the
beginning of April, 1614, the Constable died at
the Château of La Grange near Pézénas. In his
decline the debauched old man had begun to
show some signs of repentance for his misdeeds
and expressed a wish to meet his death and be
interred in the Franciscan habit. He spoke of
this intention to a friend of his, one Mondragon,
who gravely agreed with him as to the wisdom of
such a course. "Faith," he exclaimed, "that is
clever of you, for if you do not disguise yourself
well, you will never enter into Paradise."[1] As
a consequence of his father's death the Duc de
Montmorency was obliged to proceed to Languedoc
to take over the governorship. He did not think
fit to take his wife with him, and except for occasional brief visits he remained separated from
her for more than a year.

The Duchess would have preferred to retire
to the Château of Chantilly during his absence,
but the Queen would not allow her to do so and
insisted upon her remaining at Court.[2] Marie de
Medici had at once conceived a genuine affection
for her godchild and kept her with her as much as
possible. Moreover, she had become truly impressed by her intelligence and said of her that
although when one looked at her one could see

[1] Tallemant des Réaux.   [2] Cotolendi, 8.

that she was actually only fifteen, when one heard her speak one would think she was thirty.[1] Marie Félice did not, however, attempt to turn her brains to political advantage, although there would have been countless opportunities of doing so had she wished. She avoided politics like the plague, to the great amusement of the Queen, who to tease her would insist upon her remaining in the room while she was holding the Council. Marie Félice hated this and would always escape as soon as she could. "Opportunities to leave my room seem to grow beneath your feet as soon as business is talked of before me," said the Queen once, "and yet I believe you to be just as capable as those who do direct it."[2]

It was inevitable that her intelligence and personality should impress others besides the Queen, and, owing to the lofty position held by her husband and also to a belief that she might be able to exploit the Queen's affection for her in gaining political influence, many efforts were made by the ambitious to gain an ascendancy over her. Particularly forward in such endeavours was Leonora Galigai, the Florentine wife of Concini, Maréchal d'Ancre, the adventurer who was then in favour with the Queen-Regent. Her object was to gain through his wife the friendship of Montmorency, who had declared himself to be

---

[1] Rénée, 16; Monlaur, 29.   [2] Rénée, 16.

implacably opposed to the Maréchal d'Ancre.
But although La Galigai tried all her arts on the
young girl, speaking Italian to her and trying to
enlist her sympathy by playing upon the mutual
bond they had in their country of origin, Marie
Félice remained so unresponsive that La Galigai
complained to the Queen of her coldness. It did
not even avail her to praise Montmorency to his
wife and to hold out great hopes for his future.
Marie Félice snubbed her most effectively with
the proud statement that all she desired was that
the Duke her husband should preserve the honour
which his birth and virtue had acquired for him.[1]

Equally unsuccessful were the efforts of the
Maréchal de Marillac to involve her in political
intrigues. Although, by advancing her youth and
inexperience as reasons for her refusal, she tried
to avoid giving offence and making enemies, she
remained obstinately determined to do nothing
which could possibly commit her husband. It
was, indeed, only at Montmorency's own urgent
request, that she on one sole occasion made use of
the influence she might have wielded at Court.
This was when in 1616 she petitioned for and
secured the release of her brother-in-law, the
Duc d'Angoulême, who had been in prison for
twelve years. Marie de Medici had promised to

---

[1] For these efforts to entrap Marie Félice see Cotolendi, 9; Baillon,
37; Rénée, 6; Monlaur, 30.

D

release Angoulême on the occasion of Montmorency's marriage, but had been persuaded by
Concini to break her word.[1]

While her husband was away, Marie Félice,
on the plea that she was in mourning for the Constable, led a quiet and retired life and avoided
social functions as much as possible. She chose
to spend much of her time with her sisters-in-law
the Duchesses of Angoulême and Ventadour,
since with them she could talk to her heart's content of the husband whom she adored. At all
other times she was silent and sad and reserved.
"We have only half of Madame de Montmorency,"
said the Queen, "her body is with us, but her heart
is in Languedoc."[2]

She made use of the abundant leisure she had
at this time in endeavouring to learn French, for
she had known very little when she first came to
the country. When Henri first went to Languedoc
she had not even known enough to be able to write
to him, and for this purpose had had to employ
the secretary whom the Constable had placed
at her service on her arrival. But one post-day
when the secretary did not happen to be at hand
she ventured for the first time to essay a letter of
her own. Montmorency was delighted and at
once wrote asking her to continue, which she did.
When it got to the ears of the Court that she was

[1] Du Cros, 17.   [2] Baillon, 39-40; Monlaur, 33; Rénée, 15.

writing love-letters to her husband in French the young princesses were so thrilled and amused that they caused some of her letters to be intercepted and carried to the Queen. Marie de Medici had the decency to return them unopened, saying with a smile, "I swear to you that no one has seen them, but if there is nothing secret in them, do give us the pleasure of reading them."[1]

The Duchesse de Montmorency was scrupulously faithful to her husband both in deed and in thought, and in fact carried her resentment of harmless liberties to a somewhat absurd length. One day during a ball at Court her brother-in-law, the Prince de Condé, playfully insisted upon removing her gloves in order that her beautiful hands might be revealed. She suffered him to do so because of his near relationship, but declared at the same time that she would never allow such a liberty to anyone else. The King was told of what she had said, and, coming up to her, laughingly remarked: "I too would pull off your gloves if I liked." Marie Félice answered: "Sire, I would not allow it." But since Louis XIII looked rather annoyed she hastily added: "Sire, your Majesty knows well that I would never put you to the trouble of doing so." Her ready tact saved the situation. Louis laughed and remarked to the bystanders: "You see, you can never catch her

[1] Monlaur, 35–6.

out, whatever she says." The King appears, indeed, to have been more than a little enamoured of her and had a great respect for her intelligence and learning, affectionately nicknaming her '*La Sage*'[1]

Although there were all sorts of functions going on at Court at this time which might have been expected to appeal to a girl of her age, Marie Félice remained singularly indifferent to them all. She cared little for the festivities and pageants held to celebrate the majority of the King and the holding of the Estates General. Her only real pleasure was in the few fleeting visits her husband was able to make to her every now and then.

When the Court went south to Bordeaux in November, 1615, to escort the Princess Elizabeth of France, who was to marry the Infant of Spain, and to receive in return Louis XIII's Spanish bride, Anne of Austria, the Duc de Montmorency was still in Languedoc; but he made an unexpected appearance in Bordeaux to the amazement and joy of his wife who swooned away at the sight of him.[2] Her custom of expressing in this manner any strong emotion, whether of joy, sorrow, or merely surprise, must have proved embarrassing and even unnerving to the Duke on many occasions.

The Duc and Duchesse de Montmorency attended the ceremony of the exchange of

[1] Baillon, 31; Rénée, 16; Monlaur, 35.   [2] Rénée, 21; Baillon, 43.

princesses and that of the King's wedding and
then accompanied the Court back to Paris. This
journey was a harrowing experience for the tender-
hearted Marie Félice. The winter was unusually
severe and the poverty-stricken peasantry were
dying of cold and hunger in the country through
which they had to pass. The respect of the Court
for the Duchesse de Montmorency was increased
by the generosity and solicitude which she showed
for the poor and suffering. At Poitiers she heard
the news of the deaths in rapid succession of her
father and of one of her brothers, Cardinal Orsini.
The shock was so great that she fell seriously
ill. Montmorency was assiduous in his attentions
to her, while the Queen Regent also refused to
leave her and would not proceed back to Paris
until she was sufficiently recovered to travel.

Except for a few rapid journeys to Languedoc
in the spring and autumn of 1616 Montmorency
now remained with his wife for more than a year.
They divided their time between the Court in
Paris and their Château of Chantilly, and this
was a period of great happiness for both of them.
Marie Félice had from the first conceived a passion
for her husband which absorbed almost her whole
being. Everywhere he went she would follow
him about with her eyes. So profoundly did
she feel all that concerned him that at times when
he was in danger she would always fall ill. Her

love for him even caused qualms in her deeply religious mind, for sometimes she felt as if it was causing her to neglect God. At such moments she would refuse to allow him to accompany her to mass on the ground that his very presence took her mind off divine thoughts.[1] In mundane matters she was inclined to spoil him, pandering to his taste for magnificence by having the most splendid clothes made for him without his knowledge and giving her own jewels to adorn them. She was eager for him always to outshine all others present, but she herself, although she possessed excellent taste in dress, cared little for such things, beautifying herself only to please her husband and attiring herself in the most simple and unostentatious fashion whenever he was not there to see her.[2]

By this time the ascendancy of the Maréchal d'Ancre had begun to arouse serious discontent all over the country, and when the Prince de Condé was arrested and imprisoned by his orders open revolt broke out. The country speedily became involved in a civil war. While an army under Montigny was ravaging the Nivernais, the Duc de Guise was besieging Nevers and Mayenne in Soissons. In the circumstances Montmorency determined to enter into an arrangement with the Ducs d'Épernon and Lesdiguières to raise an

[1] Monlaur, 23-4.   [2] Montpensier, III, 351; Monlaur, 47.

army to relieve Soissons, declare for the King, and oust Concini from his counsels.[1] This project was rendered unnecessary by the murder of the hated favourite in April, 1617.

At the time of the murder Montmorency was in Languedoc, where he had gone for the purpose of holding the Estates at Béziers and recruiting his army. He did not attempt to disguise his pleasure at the removal of a man whom he had always regarded as an upstart and an adventurer and gave a purse of fifty golden crowns to the messengers who brought him the news.[2]

The murder of d'Ancre did not, however, bring about the change that had been hoped, for he was succeeded in his position of royal favourite by Luynes, a man of much the same calibre. As he did not trouble to conceal his enmity for Montmorency, whose lofty position and high rank he viewed with jealousy, the Duke resolved to remain for a while in Languedoc, where he could feel himself in perfect security. The Montmorencys were almost petty princes in this southern province. 'The character of the House of Montmorency, which for a long time had been governors of Languedoc,' says Cardinal Richelieu, 'was so impressed upon this people that they thought the name of King imaginary.'[3]

[1] Du Cros, 18; Bassompierre, II, 92.
[2] Monlaur, 52.
[3] Richelieu, *Mémoires* (Mich et Pouj) VIII, 419

CHAPTER III

Marie Félice joins the Duke in Languedoc—Her entry into Montpellier—Montmorency's generosity and extravagance—He entrusts money matters to his wife —His enormous household—Marie Félice tries in vain to cut it down—He transfers his superfluous pages to her service—Stories of Montmorency's lavishness— Marie Félice beloved in Languedoc—La Grange des Prés—Marie Félice for once loses her temper—Montmorency's enemies at Court—The Ballet of True Love —The Duke's infidelity—His many amours—Mademoiselle de Choisy—The Princesse de Guéménée—The Marquis de Sablé—Montmorency supposed to be in love with Anne of Austria—The Duchess's singular attitude towards the Duke's amours—Her answer to a complaining wife—Insolence of an Italian maid-of-honour—Marie Félice wins her husband to comparative fidelity—Their grief at the lack of an heir.

Since Montmorency now proposed to stay in Languedoc indefinitely, it was decided in the spring of 1617 that Marie Félice should join him there,[1] and she set out under the escort of her brother, Cosimo Orsini, to pay her first visit to the seat of her husband's government. They were met at Beaucaire by a deputation of notables from Montpellier headed by the Bishop of Lavaur. The Duchess answered their compliments modestly

[1] In his history of Montpellier D'Aigrefeuille makes the mistake of placing this visit in the year 1615.

but briefly, her knowledge of French not being
even yet very considerable. At Pézénas Montmorency joined his wife for her formal entrance
into Montpellier, but he regarded this occasion
as pre-eminently hers and endeavoured to efface
himself as much as possible, thrusting her into
the foreground and causing her to reply to all the
addresses made to them.

On June the 18th they dined at the Château
de Boutonnet, a short distance outside Montpellier, and at four o'clock they proceeded into
the town itself. Fifteen boys habited as Amazons
escorted the open litter in which the Duchess was
borne, while five hundred of the nobility and the
citizens in force came out to meet them. The
streets were lined with arquebusiers and pikemen,
and the civic dignitaries in their scarlet robes
awaited them at the gate of the city. As the
procession passed beneath the gateway a fanfare
of trumpets sounded from above and salvoes of
artillery thundered forth. Progress was exceedingly slow, for at every moment a halt was called
in order that someone might make a speech or
recite a poem. The citizens had erected no less
than six magnificent and elaborate triumphal
arches covered with heraldic and emblematic
devices and graced with mottoes replete with
recondite classical and historical allusions. One
of the devices represented a rose tree flowering

among onions with the legend '*Oppositis Fragrantior Exit*'. The rose was an allusion to one of the armorial bearings of the Orsini family, and to Marie Félice, who certainly was not conceited about her looks, it must have been some satisfaction to know that in the eyes of the good people of Montpellier she at least compared favourably with the onion.

At the portal of the church of Notre Dame they were welcomed with music from the clergy and an oration from the Bishop of Montpellier. There is no record of his speech, but many of the other odes and poems delivered on this occasion have been printed—and many of them are very long. After they left the church a special welcome to the Duchess on behalf of the ladies of Montpellier was made by three nymphs representing the deities of the river, the woods, and the hills, who begged her acceptance of a casket of wonderful jewels. She was also presented with a grant from the Estates of three thousand crowns, which she immediately distributed in charity.[1] Altogether the festivities lasted for a week and included banquets, ballets, and a pastoral interlude performed in the Langue d'Oc by the medical students, which, though very complimentary, must have been totally incomprehensible to Marie Félice.[2]

---

[1] Baillon, 36.

[2] This account is taken from *Entrée de Madame de Montmaurensi à Montpellier*, 1617.

Montmorency possessed that amiable distaste
for simple mathematics which so often characterizes
the open-handed. His generosity was surpassed
by his carelessness and he was only too pleased to
entrust all matters concerning money to his wife,
whose good sense he held in the utmost respect.
Her own household was so admirably regulated
that he requested her to endeavour to produce the
same sort of order in his. But his prodigality was
such that she found the task well-nigh impossible.
His following was enormous, especially as in add-
tion to his own household he had taken on that of
his father, the Constable, in its entirety after his
death.[1] He was surrounded by a retinue almost
as numerous as and much more brilliant than that
of the King. No less than a hundred gentlemen
constantly followed him and were maintained at
his expense. The Duchess was for ever remon-
strating with him about his extravagance, but
could never make him see reason. Nevertheless,
there was no element of bitterness in their dis-
cussions on such subjects; they were always
conducted with the utmost good humour on both
sides.

In order to bring down expenses within some
sort of bounds Marie Félice suggested to her
husband that they should try to cut down his
household. The Duke replied that he was always

---

[1] Pitaval, 21.

willing to listen to reason and asked her to furnish
him with a list of all those servants who in her
opinion might be dismissed. But for every one
that she mentioned he found some sort of an
excuse or justification, and failing anything else
would say: "If he is useless to-day, he might be
indispensable to-morrow." There were, however,
just two for keeping whom he could find no sort
of reason. The Duchess urged him to dismiss at
least these. But the Duke turned to her with a
whimsical smile: "Are they not unfortunate
enough in being useless without our adding this
misfortune in addition?" When she persisted, he
said: "Dear heart, let us then share the disagree-
able task: do you first give notice to one of them,
then I will send the other away." Of course in
the end both of them stayed.

Another story relates that the Duchess went to
her husband and pointed out to him that it was
scarcely right that he should keep twenty-four
pages while she contented herself with six. Montmorency gravely agreed with her, but instead of
dismissing his superfluous pages as she had intended him to do, he called them to him and
informed them that from this time onwards they
were to regard themselves as being in the service
of the Duchess.

In view of Montmorency's character all such
attempts at economy were predestined to failure.

Marie Félice too was in reality quite as generous
as her husband, though at first she did at least
show a little more discrimination in her charities,
confining her gifts to those who seemed to deserve
them. But Montmorency soon removed the last
vestiges of her common sense. One day she was
driving with him when they were accosted by
several apparently able-bodied men who demanded
alms from them. Marie Félice refused, telling
them that they ought to work instead of wasting
the day in begging; but Montmorency threw
them a piece of gold and whispered in his wife's
ear: "My heart, you must not think of them,
but of God in whose name they ask." The inevitable result of such behaviour on his part was that
Marie Félice soon became as reckless in charity
as himself.

If Montmorency was indiscriminate in his giving
he possessed at the same time the art of giving
gracefully. On one occasion when he was gambling
and some twenty thousand crowns lay on the table
before him, a poor gentleman among the onlookers
whispered to one of the Duke's officers that far
less than that sum would suffice to restore his
shattered fortunes. Montmorency appeared not to
have heard him and went on playing cards—and
winning. But a little later when the game was
over he dismissed everyone and, calling the gentleman to him, pushed all the money across the table

to him, saying with a smile: "I only wish, Sir, that I had been able to make a still greater fortune for you."

Another time when he was riding with several other gentlemen in the country the talk happened to turn on the subject of the nature of happiness. They chanced to meet some labourers and Montmorency remarked: "I would like to know if those men are really happy." Accordingly, without revealing his identity, he accosted them and put the question to them. Two of them replied that they were happy enough, since they had good masters and wives and families whom they loved and whom they were able to keep in comfort with the money they earned by their labours. The third, however, replied that he had unfortunately run into debt, and that his little piece of land had had to be sold to pay his creditors. If only he possessed fifty pistoles to buy it back again he would be completely happy. "Well," said the Duke, "for once in my life I shall have had the pleasure of making somebody happy," and he made his squire pay the man fifty pistoles there and then before he mounted his horse and rode away.

Montmorency took a fantastic pride in his splendid extravagance. Once when the Duchess, having made up the accounts, as she was wont, and finding in them one wholly excessive item,

came to him and begged him to mitigate his
extravagance, he asked her for the register and
wrote upon it: 'Why am I not an Emperor that I
might give still more?' This disposition can
only have been further stimulated by a remark
once made to him by a Spanish grandee, the
Duque de Osuna, who, dazzled by his magnificence,
exclaimed: "Nature has made a mistake: she
made you only a duke, but designed you for a
king."

The Duke was adored in Languedoc, and Marie
Félice speedily became as beloved as her husband.
Her charity, wisdom, and justice caused the people
to bring their disputes before her and ask her to
act as peace-maker. So successful was she in such
matters that the Duke would leave to her all those
that were referred to him and would rally her
gaily on her judicial functions. "How many
decisions have you pronounced since I last saw
you?" he would ask.

For those who were thrown into prison for whatever reason the Duchess had the deepest sympathy,
and it was her invariable habit to release all
debtors by settling their debts. Her unfailing
pity for the unfortunate was inclined to be an
embarrassment to the Duke at times when severity
was absolutely essential. No execution could ever
take place in a town where she was, and if it was
necessary that the sentence should be carried

out, it had to be deferred till she was out of
the way.

Although the Montmorencys possessed several
residences in Languedoc they spent most of their
time at a country-house called La Grange des
Prés built by the Constable on the bank of the
river Hérault not far from the town of Pézénas.
This was said to be the loveliest house in
Languedoc and the one in the loveliest surroundings. Here they led a life full of gaiety. There
were constant festivities of all kinds; races, games,
tournaments, reunions of the nobility, and splendid
balls followed one another in rapid succession.
Marie Félice was a beautiful dancer, but would
never attend balls except when the Duke could be
present.

Montmorency was passionately fond of cards
and a great deal of playing went on at their house.
It was on one of these occasions that occurred
the only recorded instance when the gentle Marie
Félice really lost her temper. The most extraordinary good luck had followed her all the evening
and it did not seem as if she could make a single
error. A certain gentleman who was present had
the bad taste to murmur, whether seriously or not,
that she must have been looking at the cards of
the other players. The remark so infuriated
Marie Félice that she swept the cards and the

stakes off the table with such force that the money rolled all over the floor and some of the cards even got stuck edgewise in the cracks between the floor-boards. Her fury, however, was of short duration, for a little later she sent for the gentleman who had caused this outburst and apologized to him for her display of temper. This incident had a sequel. One day when the Duchess had gently reproached someone in her suite for losing their temper, Montmorency, who loved to tease her, whispered in her ear: "My heart, do you remember the day when the cards got stuck in the floor-boards?" Marie Félice's reply made the Duke blush in his turn: "It is not fair to remember what you have seen only once."[1]

Montmorency's very popularity produced for him countless enemies, especially at Court, where there were many who were only too anxious to do him all the ill offices in their power. Foremost amongst his detractors was Luynes, who lost no opportunity of insinuating calumnies about him into the ears of the King. So engaging was his personality and so winning were his manners that when he actually appeared at Court he was usually able to confound his traducers and disperse the cloud of unkind rumours that had clustered about him

[1] The preceding anecdotes of the Duke and Duchess are taken from the following sources: Cotolendi, 24; Desormeaux, 203, 205, 454–5; Monlaur, 61–3; 65–6; 69–70; 73–4; Rénée, 20–1; Baillon, 101–2; Pitaval, 24–5; 282–5.

E

during his absence; but as soon as he left Court
the favour he enjoyed there disappeared also and
his critics gained the upper hand.   When he went
to Court in 1618 he found it impossible immediately
to dispel the prejudice his enemies had cumulated
against him during his long absence in Languedoc.
He met with a frigid reception from the King, and
the coldness and dissatisfaction with which he was
regarded showed themselves in overt acts, not of
great importance in themselves perhaps, but galling
because indicative of royal disfavour.   Thus he was
cut to the heart when the King refused him the
governorship of Tarascon, which ordinarily would
have been his for the asking.   When he returned
to Languedoc Marie Félice did all that she could
to divert him in his chagrin and endeavoured to
persuade him to forget his grievances in the festivities he loved so well.   She caused a magnificent
'Ballet of True Love' to be performed before him
at La Grange des Prés.[1]

'True Love' the Duchess certainly felt for her
husband.   She adored him and him only; never
once did the breath of scandal touch her name.
It is regrettable to have to record that it was far
otherwise with the Duke her husband.   He was
consistently unfaithful to her.   Mademoiselle de
Montpensier states that he was one of the most
'gallant' men of his time.[2]   Such excuse as there

[1] Monlaur, 94.   [2] Montpensier, III, 351.

may be for infidelity he possessed. Besides that
he himself was by nature and heredity of hot
blood and amorous inclinations the examples of
his father, the Constable, and his godfather,
Henri IV, had scarcely been calculated to inspire
in him a lofty view of the opposite sex. It might,
indeed, almost be said that his very upbringing
militated against chastity. Moreover, temptations
were abundant. Apart from his rank and riches
he was in himself a romantic figure, handsome,
brave, elegant, and generous, and one of the best
dancers and riders in France. It was little wonder
that every woman with a disposition for gallantry
set her cap at him. Tallemant des Réaux even
goes so far as to say that women who had never
set eyes on him came from the provinces with
the avowed intention of making him their
lover.

Of his love-intrigues when in Languedoc and
away from Court little is known except that he
had them and that they were many. But some
of his affairs with ladies of the Court attained
a greater notoriety. His first serious love was
for Mademoiselle de Choisy, and he also had a
passionate affair with Anne de Rohan, Princesse
de Guéménée, who appears to have thrown herself successfully at his head after she had been
jilted by the Comte de Soissons. A ribald rhyme
was made on her rapid recovery.

Belle de Guéménée,
Soissons vous a laissée
Avec son inconstance ;
Mais les yeux de travers
Vous ont mise à l'envers.[1]

Montmorency's squint was too well-known to leave any doubt as to the identity of the Princess's new lover. Anne de Guéménée is said to have brought ill luck to all her lovers; it is certain that four of them at any rate, Soissons, Bouteville, De Thou, and Montmorency came to a tragic end. She appears always to have retained an affectionate remembrance of Montmorency, and it is related that she fell to the ground in a dead faint when his shield was removed at the ceremony of making knights at Fontainebleau shortly after his death.[2]

The most notorious of all his love-affairs was that with Madeleine de Souvré, Marquise de Sablé,[3] who was one of the foremost '*précieuses*' of the Hôtel de Rambouillet and was as beautiful as she was brilliant. According to Tallemant des Réaux it was simply through vanity that she

---

[1] Quoted by Baillon, 65.

[2] Tallemant des Réaux,

[3] Madeleine de Souvré (1599–1678) married 1614 to Philippe-Emmanuel de Laval-Montmorency, Marquis de Sablé.   Her biographer, V. Cousin, says that there are no details extant as to the period and duration of the liaison.   According to him, Montmorency was her only love, ' and after Montmorency we perceive no more than a well-marked sentiment, friendship.' Cousin, *Madame de Sablé*, 1854, p. 11.

first sought Montmorency's favours, since his
strange indifference to her varied charms had
well-nigh maddened her. But in truth it is more
likely that she was strongly attracted by his gay
and gallant youthfulness. When he vaulted
through the window on his first visit to her he
leapt straight into her heart. The liaison, which
began when she was very young, lasted for some
considerable time and was renewed at intervals.
The beautiful Marquise appears to have been
furiously jealous of her lover and on one occasion
made him a scene because, she said, he preferred
to dance always with the prettiest women at the
balls at the Louvre. She ordered him henceforth
to dance only with the ugliest ones; but in view
of his disposition it is improbable that he obeyed
her.

She seems to have been an exacting mistress.
The Duke had once promised to visit her at her
Château of Sablé in Maine on his way back from
Languedoc, although it was well out of his way.
On the news of his approach she sent a gentleman
to him to inform him that she was impatiently
awaiting him. The gentleman returned with the
message that the Duke on his part was burning
to see her. Madame de Sablé then enquired what
the Duke had been doing when the messenger
reached him. "Madame," replied her emissary,
"the inns at the place where he was having

dinner were not very good, and he was obliged to send to some sportsmen in the neighbourhood to bring him two partridges. He had them prepared in his presence, watched them being roasted, and ate them with excellent appetite." Madame de Sablé was so disgusted that the Duke should be able at such a time to think of any other food than that of love that when he arrived she flatly refused to receive him.[1]

To her credit be it recorded that, although she was his mistress, Madame de Sablé steadfastly refused to accept any of the valuable presents which Montmorency was eager to shower on her. She herself put an end to the affair at last when she perceived that the Duke's passion was cooling and imagined that he had fallen in love with the Queen. Then from sheer pride and no other motive, as she herself admitted to Madame de Motteville, she refused to have anything more to do with him.

Although it was freely rumoured that Montmorency was, or at least professed to be, in love with Louis XIII's queen, it is more probable that he possessed for her nothing more than a chivalrous and romantic devotion free from any ulterior thoughts. Anne of Austria herself told Madame de Motteville that she had never thought seriously of Montmorency's feelings towards her

[1] Tallemant des Réaux.

and that she had regarded all that public report
had credited him with as a tribute that she
considered due to her from everyone, being persuaded that his passion for her had never been
genuine.[1]

Nevertheless, the whole story was much bruited
about at the time. It was told thinly disguised by
Mademoiselle de Scudéri in her romance *Le Grand
Cyrus*.[2] Montmorency figured there as Polydamas
and Madame de Sablé as Parthenice. The poet
Voiture, under the name of Callicrate, clever as
a monkey, but less endowed with looks, charm,
and rank than his rival, used all his endeavours
to supplant Polydamas in the affections of
Parthenice, trying to prove that he was lacking
in wit by concealing himself during one of the
lovers' meetings, taking down their conversation,
and afterwards presenting the lady with a copy
of the result to show her that everything that
had been worth saying had been said by her.
But the plot failed, for nothing could lessen
Parthenice's passion for Polydamas until she herself imagined that he had played her false by
declaring himself *Chevalier de la Reine*.[3]

Montmorency never attempted to conceal from
his wife that he was being unfaithful to her, and

[1] Motteville, 12–14.
[2] *Artamène ou Le Grand Cyrus*, written by Madalène de Scudéri
but published under the name of her brother, Georges.
[3] For Montmorency's affair with Madame de Sablé see especially
Baillon, 66 *et seq.*

according to Tallemant des Réaux the Duchess, though jealous, would never protest so long as her husband was quite open in his amours. Her attitude in the matter was most singular. She herself was so attracted by him that she seemed to feel a sort of secret sympathy with the other women who fell victims to his charm.[1] At times when she was aware that he was going to an amorous appointment she would place some new ribbon, scarf, or lace with his clothes for his better adornment. When he came home she would welcome him with smiles, and if he made excuses for being away so long she would say: "I do not wish to oppose your pleasures, nor do I think ill of you; but you have God and your conscience as your judges—do not offend them."[2] It was apparently on principle that she refrained from reproaches, for she said once to a woman who complained that her husband was unfaithful to her: "With the help of silence you can get over everything, you must not speak of this sort of grief save to God alone." Nevertheless, his infidelities did fill her with a sorrow so profound that occasionally even Montmorency himself would notice it. On one such occasion he said to her: "What is wrong with you? You seem to me quite changed." "That is true," she answered sadly, "but my heart is not, and that must satisfy

[1] Montpensier, III, 351.   [2] Monlaur, 83

you." Her gentleness was for ever recalling Montmorency's wandering affections; he would profess
extreme penitence, but it would not last long, and
a few days later he was always off again on some
new intrigue.[1]

One of the incidents that must have been most
distressing to the Duchess was when her husband
was attracted by one of her own maids-of-honour,
an Italian girl with a beautiful voice. Montmorency would spend hours alone with her, listening
to her singing. With her usual tact Marie Félice
was scrupulously careful to avoid finding them
together. Unfortunately the Duke's attentions made
the girl grow proud and she made so bold as
to treat the Duchess with ill-mannered arrogance.
The rest of the Duchess's attendants were so
furious that their beloved mistress should be so
insulted that they wanted to make representations to the Duke to have the girl dismissed.
Some even threatened to seize her and throw
her into the Rhone at Lyons, where this incident
took place. But the Duchess got to hear of their
projects and would not allow them to interfere.
In view of her admirable forbearance it is pleasant
to be able to record that long afterwards the girl
herself repented and humbly craved the Duchess's
forgiveness.[2]

[1] Cotolendi, 27; Desormeaux, 207; Rénée, 23; Monlaur, 81–2.
[2] Rénée, 23–4; Monlaur, 84.

The gentle restraint of Marie Félice did not fail in the end to make its impression on the Duke. From the first he had always possessed a deep and abiding affection for her and had always been delicate and considerate in his attentions to her, but in the course of time his affectionate respect deepened into a real love. He openly announced that he had been reclaimed by his wife's charm and virtue and swore that in future he would love no one but her. It is doubtful whether he kept this promise to the letter, but at any rate from this time onwards his infidelities were less frequent and less conspicuous, and those ladies for whom he professed ephemeral passions had more cause to be jealous of Marie Félice than she had to be jealous of them. His heart was hers alone and hers irrevocably. In the fervour of his renascent love he once said to his sister, the Princesse de Condé: "I used to say: I love my sister best and then my wife. Now I have to say: I love my wife best and then my sister."[1]

Marie Félice was so overjoyed at regaining her husband's love that she tried to make some return to God for sending him back to her, and could think of no better way than to deprive herself of Henri's presence for several hours to go and pray at Christmas. As she was on her way to the

---

[1] Monlaur, 87–8.

PLATE II

MARGVERITE CHARLOTE DE MONTMORENCI
PRINCESSE DE CONDE PR. PRINCESSE DV SANG.

Par son tres-humbleseruiteur Balt. Moncornet.   *Auec Priuilege.*

chapel Montmorency met her and took her in his
arms. "To-day we will go and make our
devotions together," he said. But his wife tore
herself from his grasp and fled, crying: "Today,
my soul, I shall leave you for God!"[1] The poor
Duke was left standing dumbfounded in the
passage. It is perhaps fortunate that the Duchess
could never again summon up enough strength
of spirit to repeat her sacrifice!

Even though Marie Félice was now happy in
her husband's love, she could not bring herself
to forget the past entirely, and sometimes
Montmorency would find her pensive and melan-
choly. Divining the cause, he would say: "My
heart, if you cannot forget the past, consider that
had I been better, you would have been less good;
for how many rosaries must you have said for
me!"[2]

Both to Montmorency and to Marie Félice it was
an abiding grief that no heir had been vouchsafed
to them. Marie Félice in particular felt that she
was betraying the illustrious house of Montmorency
in failing to provide it with an heir. She was
aware that the sterility was attributed to her, since
Montmorency already had an illegitimate son in
Languedoc by a pretty girl from Béziers known
as 'La Fortune'.[3] In her ardent desire she would

[1] Monlaur, 89.   [2] Baillon, 74; Monlaur, 87.
[3] Desormeaux, 318n; Pitaval, 24.

spend hours in prayer and once went on a pilgrimage to a shrine of Our Lady in Languedoc. She walked for a whole day and arrived so exhausted and with her bare feet so cut about that she was unable to stir from her bed for three days.[1]

Although Montmorency felt the misfortune of having no heir as acutely as did his wife, he always attempted to deceive her as to his true feelings, assuring her that his happiness was complete and he desired no more in the world.   His whole household had strict injunctions never to mention the subject to their mistress, and he himself would rarely allude to it save in the lightest way, as once when she was reproaching him for some extravagance he said: "Thank God we have no children; if we had, you would pension me off and I should have to take to stealing!"[2]

[1] Monlaur, 91.
[2] Monlaur, 91; Rénée, 33–4; Baillon, 75–6.

CHAPTER IV

A progress through Languedoc—Tournament at
Toulouse—Marie de Medici escapes from Blois—Montmorency saves Lord Herbert from making a fool of
himself—He receives the Order of the Saint Esprit—
Religious troubles in Languedoc—Privas occupied by
the Huguenots—Montmorency tries peaceful persuasion
—Surrender of Privas—Luynes calumniates Montmorency—The King and his mother once more at
loggerheads—Marie de Medici appeals to Montmorency
—Marie Félice persuades him to remain loyal to the
King—The King's frigid reception of Montmorency—
Affection of the troops for Montmorency—Privas re-
captured by the Huguenots—Montmorency advances
on Privas—His bravery before Vals—He takes Valons
and other places—He joins the King before Montauban
—Luynes' jealousy of Montmorency—Montmorency's
illness causes the troops to desert—Abandonment of
the siege—Gravity of the Duke's illness—Marie Félice
hastens to his bedside—His miraculous recovery—
Death of Luynes—The Duc de Lesdiguieres made
Constable — Montmorency's disappointment — Summer
campaign of 1622—Montmorency at the siege of Montpellier— His gallant exploit there—The Montmorencys
return to Paris.

In January, 1619, the Duc and Duchesse de
Montmorency made a progress through those parts
of Languedoc which the Duchess had not yet
visited. She was greeted at Béziers, Narbonne,
Carcassonne, Castelnaudary, and Toulouse with the
same elaborate pageantry as had graced her first

entry into Montpellier. At Toulouse they made a prolonged stay and all the nobility of the neighbourhood flocked into the town and formed a court around them. When Montmorency received news that the marriage of the King's sister to the Prince of Piedmont had been fixed for the 10th of February he arranged that a two days' tournament should be held to celebrate the occasion. 'The better to prepare themselves for these rejoicings,' says the chronicler of the *Mercure François*, 'they began by a Ballet.'

At the tournament Marie Félice was seated in the place of honour at the end of the lists while Montmorency himself took part in the tilting and riding at the ring. Montmorency had provided three bouquets of diamond flowers as prizes on the opening day. The first, for the victor in the tilting, was won by the Baron de Savignac, the second, for the most gorgeous appearance, by Montmorency himself, and the third, for the most original and ingenious costume, by the Marquis de Portes as a mad knight in a fantastic costume covered with silver bells. The winners all gallantly presented their awards to 'three of the most beautiful damsels in this great assembly.' The riding at the ring on the following day was won by the Sieur de Pins whom Marie Félice crowned with laurel and presented with a fine diamond of great value.[1]

[1] *Mercure*, 1619, V, 108-127.

Scarcely were these celebrations over before the news reached Languedoc that with the help of the Duc d'Épernon Queen Marie de Medici had made her escape from the Castle of Blois, where she had been confined, and was starting to rally a party round her near Angers. During the disputes which ensued between the King and his mother Montmorency wisely decided to remain quietly in Languedoc and avoid taking sides. Civil war was on the point of breaking out when Richelieu, then Bishop of Luçon, succeeded in negotiating a peace between the mother and son by the Treaty of Angoulême, (April, 1619). But it was not until the autumn that the Duc and Duchesse de Montmorency ventured to return to Paris.

It was probably during this journey that there took place a certain incident related by Lord Herbert of Cherbury in his autobiography. Herbert, an extraordinarily hot-headed and disputatious man, while at Lyons quarrelled with the Governor, the Marquis de St. Chaumont, to whom, even according to his own account, he appears to have been exceedingly and unnecessarily uncivil. At any rate his intimate friend, Sir Edward Sackville, actually refused to second him when he sent a challenge to the Governor. As Montmorency was passing through Lyons on his way to Paris he heard what had happened and, knowing Herbert of old, was kind-hearted enough to intervene to extract him from his undignified position. He sent his own guards for him and went with him to the Governor, whom by some means he prevailed upon to offer an apology for the misunderstanding that had arisen. He then told Herbert that with this he should be satisfied. But Herbert was so touchy about his dignity that he still hung back until he had received the Duke's solemn assurance that he himself would have been satisfied in like case.

Montmorency's loyalty during this difficult year had substantially increased his credit at Court, and in January, 1620, Louis XIII conferred on him the grand cordon of the Order of the Saint Esprit. With her usual generosity Marie Félice gave some of her best jewels to adorn his mantle.[1]

While Montmorency was in Paris serious dissensions arose between Catholics and Protestants in Languedoc and he had to set off post-haste, leaving Marie Félice behind him at Chantilly. The first spark had been set alight at Privas. The daughter and heiress of the family of Chambaud, which held the lordship of Privas, married the Vicomte de L'Estrange, who, as was customary, by his marriage became Governor of the town. But L'Estrange was both a Catholic and a personal enemy of Brison, the Huguenot leader, and the town being fervently Protestant refused to admit him. He dared not go openly to and from the

[1] Monlaur, 97

Château by the main gateway, but was obliged
to slip in and out by a small postern and often
enough even to fight his way through that. Every
evening the inhabitants used to collect beneath
the windows of the connubial bedchamber making
the night hideous by shouting and yelling insults
and singing ribald songs.[1] Naturally enough feeling soon began to run high between the two
factions and riots ensued.

The Huguenots, incited by their clergy and led
by Brison, attacked the Château, which L'Estrange
had garrisoned with some twenty-five or thirty
of his friends. L'Estrange beat them off, whereupon Brison, asserting that his resistance showed
that he possessed a dangerously violent and belli-
cose nature, thought fit to occupy the town of
Privas with four hundred men on the pretext of
protecting the inhabitants from their bloodthirsty
lord. L'Estrange appealed to Montmorency, who,
as was his wont, first tried peaceful persuasion and
sent two commissioners to endeavour to compose
the differences. The people of Privas refused even
to listen to them, and Montmorency, perceiving
that other Huguenot towns were beginning to be
affected by their contumacy, resolved upon sterner
measures. Even at this late stage he sent two
gentlemen, one Catholic and one Protestant, to
see if they could find a peaceful solution; but on

[1] Rénée, 25

F

their return they reported that Brison and the people of Privas were determined never to receive the Vicomte de L'Estrange either in the town or in the Château. Montmorency then speedily raised an army of 7,000 infantry and 300 cavalry and prepared to besiege Privas. Realizing at last that he meant business, Brison and his men hastily betook themselves off, and the inhabitants decided to give in and surrendered the place without a fight. The conditions imposed upon them by Montmorency were not hard. The Vicomte was to be suffered to pursue his matrimonial life without further molestation, and Mass was to be said once more in Privas after a lapse of sixty years. To guard against further disorders Montmorency left an officer of his own named De La Croix with 50 soldiers in charge of the Château.[1]

The Duke's enemies, ever on the watch to injure him, endeavoured to turn even a petty little success like this to his discredit. Luynes maliciously represented to the King that Montmorency had raised the troops on his own initiative without waiting for the royal authorization. But Montmorency was prepared for such criticisms and, by himself paying off the troops out of his own purse, defeated Luynes's insinuations as to the use to which he might put them.[2]   Louis XIII

---

[1] *Mercure*, 1621, VII, 180–4; Du Cros, 22 *et seq.*

[2] Monlaur, 99

later authorized him to call the Estates of
Languedoc so that they might reimburse him for
the expenses he had incurred.

The peace patched up by the Treaty of
Angoulême did not last long, and very soon the
King and the Queen-Mother were once 'more
at loggerheads. In search of support Marie de
Medici at once approached the Montmorencys,
firmly believing that she could count on Marie
Félice and knowing that Montmorency's adherence would have great influence on others. The
position was exceedingly difficult for Montmorency.
In his eyes there must have been speciousness
if not actual truth in the Queen's plea that her
party was really the King's party, because she
at least had his interests at heart, while Luynes
and his other advisers thought only of sating
their own ambitions. Nor was Marie Félice's
position any too enviable. She owed everything
to the Queen and there was a very real affection
between them. But after serious thought she
decided that the right course was to remain loyal
to the King, and she accordingly gave a frigid
reception to all Marie de Medici's emissaries who
urged her to exert her influence on her husband
to persuade him to embrace the Queen's cause.
She knew full well that this conduct would involve
her in charges of ingratitude. The Queen's friends
considered it shameful that the person who owed

most to the Queen should refuse to declare herself
on her side. Still Marie Félice remained firm,
and in all her letters to her husband who was
still in Languedoc exhorted him to remain steadfast in his allegiance.[1] One of the Queen's agents,
Du Carbon, who paid three separate visits to
Languedoc to endeavour to secure Montmorency's
adherence, put down his abstention entirely to
his wife's influence.[2] And yet, owing to the
unremitting enmity of Luynes, who insinuated
that the Duke's loyalty must be doubtful as his
wife was an Italian and niece and goddaughter
of the rebellious queen, the Court would never
trust him. The Protestant party also calumniated
him; but, as Marie Félice said, "It is a glory to
him to be wished ill for such a cause; one cannot
complain that God's enemies should be ours
also."[3]

After the defeat of the Queen-Mother and the
Duc de Retz at Ponts de Cé in August, 1620,
Louis XIII proceeded to Guienne and sent for
Montmorency, who had been at Beaucaire keeping
a watchful eye on the gathering of the Protestants
at Uzés.[4] The Duke hastened to Cadillac, but
was disappointed to receive a somewhat cold
reception from the King who had not yet got
over the mistrust with which Luynes had inspired

[1] Baillon, 79; Rénée, 27.   [3] Monlaur, 103–4.
[2] Pitaval, 30; Monlaur, 100.   [4] Du Cros, 27.

him. Nevertheless, he kept Montmorency with him during his campaign against the Protestants in Béarn and then dismissed him in order that he might return to Languedoc to hold the Estates.

Montmorency was in his element during the wars of religion that filled the next few years. A soldier by nature as well as by heredity, upbringing, and tradition, he enjoyed fighting for its own sake. It is significant that out of all his wealth his most cherished possessions were the swords of his ancestors. His men adored him and would follow him anywhere. A picturesque story is told which shows the affection almost approaching idolatry with which he was regarded by the troops. On one occasion after he had paid off some of his troops they would not leave him, but followed him from house to house in Béziers. Thinking that they wanted money, Montmorency with his usual generosity flung his purse full of gold to them from an upper window. Not a man moved forward to pick it up. They cried out that all that they wanted was to be allowed to remain with him.[1] This incident touched him profoundly. "You love these soldiers and you are pleased that I love them," he said to his wife, "but they do more for me, since they trample underfoot the money I give them."[2]

[1] Rénée, 21 ; Monlaur, 64 ; Pitaval (283 lays the scene at Montpellier).
[2] Baillon, 103 ; Pitaval, 283.

At Privas things had gone ill. While Montmorency was out of the way and L'Estrange too was absent, the inhabitants, in spite of the Duc de Ventadour's efforts for peace, had laid siege to the Château, which after holding out for a fortnight was surrendered by St. Palais, De la Croix's successor in command. Montmorency, angered that the royal authority had thus been flouted, was anxious to recapture the town, but was ordered by the King not to make the attempt unless he was certain of success. For this reason he resolved to leave nothing to chance and assured himself of having an adequate force of 3,000 infantry and 500 cavalry by pawning his own plate and jewels to raise the money to pay them. He then set forth to Privas, taking other Protestant strongholds on the way. His personal bravery was astounding and he was always in the forefront of every fight. After taking Villeneuve de Berg he proceeded against Vals, where he had a narrow escape from death, for the plume of his hat was shot off by artillery fire which killed the man next to him. On the same day, while he was reconnoitring the fortifications with the Marquis de Portes and the Sieur de Morezes, a furious musketry fire was suddenly directed upon them, and Morezes fell shot through both thighs. He earnestly requested the others to abandon him as bullets continued to fly about them, but Montmorency

flatly refused to withdraw until he had wrapped
the wounded man in his own cloak and helped to
carry him into safety. Unfortunately Morezes'
wounds were so serious that he died ten days
later.

Montmorency now contemplated making an
attack on Valons. When advised not to make
such an attempt with his small force he replied:
"The finest actions have been achieved by those
who have fought their enemies without counting
their numbers. Such was Alexander. Nothing
can stop a General who looks only to his glory."
He then made good his words by taking the fortress
in the teeth of an army under Châtillon twice as
strong as his own.

During the months of July and August Montmorency was commanded to lay waste the country
between Nîmes and Montpellier in order to deprive
the rebels of the harvest. On the 1st of July he
arrived at Conqui on the banks of the Rhone and
with his chief officers and many of the nobility
who had volunteered to serve under him took
a collation in the shade of an orchard while he
watched the arrival of his troops by boat. When
the men had disembarked they were given bread
and wine to refresh themselves and were ordered
to rest till nightfall, when an advance was made
on Marguerites, a fortified village near Nîmes.
The garrison put up a stubborn resistance and

the fighting in the streets lasted all night. Montmorency himself had several almost miraculous escapes from death. While he was changing horses owing to a broken stirrup the groom who was holding his fresh horse was shot dead by his very side.

Throughout his campaign he was being continually calumniated by those about the King, and in the end the jealousy of the Court prevented him from pressing on to Privas.[1] Instead, in the early autumn of 1621, he was summoned to join the King before Montauban, which, with La Rochelle, was one of the chief Huguenot strongholds.

Montmorency arrived at Montauban with a regiment of infantry raised at his own expense and accoutred with arms taken from a captured Dutch ship which was carrying arms for the Huguenots.[2] Luynes, now Constable of France, was in chief command of the royal forces, and his constant preoccupation to keep his own person out of all danger drew from Condé the satirical remark that, if you chose your time, Luynes was admirably fitted for any office—an excellent chancellor in time of war, and a good commander in time of peace. Luynes's hatred for Montmorency

[1] The account of the foregoing campaign is derived from *Mercure*, 1621, VII, 198–9, 694–8; Du Cros, 29, 37; Desormeaux, 217; Baillon 83; Rénée, 29; Pitaval, 33–7.
[2] Desormeaux, 218.

was so intense that he deliberately thrust him
into the positions of the greatest danger, an
arrangement eminently agreeable to the intrepid
Duke, who, as always, eagerly sought the danger-
spots at Montauban and in one of the attacks
joyously led his troops across the river under
fire to attain the breach.[1]

Shortly after the siege began Montmorency was
stricken with a contagious fever and had to be
taken to Rabastens. The discomfiture of the
army, which was already decimated by disease,
was completed by the removal of the only leader
in whom the local levies had any confidence. Now
that he was no longer with them they began to
desert and the siege had to be abandoned. Cardinal Richelieu himself attributed the collapse
of the siege largely to the disastrous effects of
Montmorency's illness,[2] and the Duke's worst
enemy, the Constable de Luynes, in a letter to the
Duc de Montbazon gave as one of the principal
reasons for the abandonment of the siege 'the
illness of Monsieur de Montmorency which caused
3,000 men whom he had brought to desert in one
night.'[3]

Montmorency's illness was long and really
serious. All the doctors, including the Duke's
own physician, the celebrated Ranchin, held out

[1]Pitaval, 39.   [2] Richelieu, *Mémoires*, (Lair) III, 162.
    [3] *Mercure*, 1621, VII, 886.

no hopes of his recovery. As soon as Marie Félice
was informed she rushed to his side from Paris
journeying day and night. When he heard of
her arrival Montmorency with his usual solicitude
asked for lumps of ice to hold in his hands so that
the violence of his fever should not frighten her.[1]
The Duchess spent hours in fervent prayer to God
to spare him. She herself afterwards related that
when one night in the agony of her spirit she cried
out: "My God, my God, are you going to take
him from me?" a mysterious heavenly voice
seemed to answer: "Not this time."[2] Somewhat
consoled by this strange happening she returned
to the sickroom, and was met at the door by the
Marquis de Portes who besought her not to enter,
as her husband was dying. At the same time he
handed her the Duke's will. The Duchess threw
it to the ground and rushed into the room, where
she found the priests already reciting the prayers
in articulo mortis. Earnestly beseeching them to
leave her husband in peace for a little while, she
sat down beside him and was overjoyed but not
surprised when before an hour had passed he took
a turn for the better. A few days later he was out
of danger, and as soon as he could travel he was
carried in a litter to Toulouse, the capital of his
government, to receive the King, who had now
become kindly disposed towards him and had

[1] Cotolendi, 32 ; Monlaur, 108–9.   [2] Baillon, 87.

frequently made anxious enquiries about him during his illness.

The Duchess claimed that the Duke's amazing recovery was due to direct intervention from on high; but others were inclined to attribute not a little to the consummate skill of the physician Ranchin. When the Duke's arch-enemy, Luynes, fell ill shortly after with the same kind of fever he sent to Montmorency asking him to lend him the services of Ranchin. This Montmorency generously did, but all Ranchin's skill did not avail to save the Constable, who died in December, 1621.[1]

While at Toulouse the King gave Montmorency chief command over all the troops in Languedoc and attached to him three thousand German troops under Schomberg's son, the Duc d'Halluin. In July, 1622, Montmorency met the King at Alzonne, near Castelnaudary, and proceeded with him to Carcassonne, where the Estates were to be held in order that it might be arranged for them to share with the King the expenses of suppressing the Huguenot rebels.

At Carcassonne Montmorency sustained a severe disappointment when the Duc de Lesdiguières, on his conversion to Roman Catholicism, was made Constable. Montmorency had hoped that this office, which until recently had been almost hereditary in his family, might be conferred on

[1] Baillon, 89 ; Monlaur, 110.

himself. Nevertheless, he accepted the disappointment with a good grace and sent St. Palais, the Captain of his Guards, to congratulate the new Constable.[1]

In the summer of 1622 Montmorency was engaged in endeavouring to counteract Rohan's operations in lower Languedoc and was on the whole successful against him, obtaining victories at Lunas, Vraysac, and Fougères. The capital, Montpellier, still obstinately refused to receive the King, and Montmorency realized that with his small forces he had no chance of taking the place. Nevertheless, he performed one bold exploit in order to show the people of Montpellier that he was a force to be reckoned with. On the night of the 2nd of July he disguised three hundred soldiers as harvesters and furnished them with carts in which arms were concealed. The next morning the people of Montpellier were greeted with the spectacle of their corn being cut before their very eyes. A body of five hundred men was sent out to expel the intruders. When the reapers saw the enemy approaching they made a hasty retreat until they came to a spot where Montmorency was waiting in concealment with his cavalry. Then they turned and fired upon their pursuers while Montmorency swept round with his horsemen and attacked them on both flanks. A hundred and fifty of them were

[1] Pitaval, 56.

killed, and nearly all the rest wounded or taken prisoners.[1]

When the King himself decided to lay siege to Montpellier, Montmorency would have wished to join him, but was commanded first to secure several other places. Of these, Aymargues surrendered on his appearance, Marsillargues capitulated on August the 4th after a three days' siege, and Sommières was taken without difficulty. Having accomplished all that he had been commanded to do, he was free to join in the siege of Montpellier, where on this occasion he received a warm welcome from the King.[2] As usual, as soon as he appeared, the young nobility of the neighbourhood flocked in to serve under him as volunteers.[3]

At the siege of Montpellier the Duke, as was his wont, deliberately chose the most dangerous posts and performed prodigies of valour. On September the 2nd he left the trenches for a while to visit his sick nephew, the Comte d'Alais, bidding his officers on no account to abandon the position during his absence. He was in the King's lodgings in conversation with His Majesty when the alarm was suddenly raised. They hurried to the window and at once perceived that the besieged had made a sally by the Bastion St.

Denis. Seeing that its defenders were being driven out, the Duke rushed forth from the royal quarters, vaulted on to the first horse he could find, and galloped off to the scene of battle practically unarmed except for his sword. The other distinguished courtiers, some twenty in all, who had bravely followed him, were killed to a man in the first charge, but Montmorency's onslaught was so terrific that the ranks of the enemy broke and fled before him alone. The royal forces, however, were so surprised and bewildered by this sudden turn in the battle that they were not immediately reassured. Thus there arose the somewhat comical situation of both sides flying from each other. Some few of Montmorency's men eventually rallied and followed him, but they were so few that the Duke himself would have been killed, had not an enemy officer chivalrously begged him to retire, since they were unwilling to slay so brave a foe in cold blood. Montmorency at length realized that he could scarcely hope to continue the fight almost single-handed, and he cut his way out of the mêlée with as much fury as he had entered it. He received two pike-wounds in this encounter, one in the chest and one in the stomach.[1]

Montmorency returned straight to the King

[1] For this incident see Du Cros, 65; *Mercure*, 1622, VIII, 814–6; Desormeaux, 227–8; Bassompierre, III, 120.

and made light of his wounds, assuring him that
they pained him much less than the thought that
the Duc de Fronsac[1] and the other brave gentlemen who had accompanied him on his desperate
sally had all lost their lives. Nevertheless, his
wounds, especially the one in the stomach, were
by no means negligible, and the King caused him
to be carried to the Duc de Chevreuse's room,
which was immediately beneath his own, and
gave orders that his own surgeons were to look
after him. Montmorency found that the noise
in these quarters worried him and hindered his
recovery, so that after a day or so his own surgeon
got leave to have him moved to Pézénas. Here
he was faithfully nursed back to health by Marie
Félice herself. He made a marvellously rapid
recovery, and, as soon as he could get about again
at the end of a fortnight, he insisted upon returning
to the siege, where he behaved as if nothing had
happened to him, spending most of his nights in
the trenches.[2]

In October, 1622, peace was made and Louis
entered Montpellier accompanied by Montmorency,
the hero of the siege. The Duke and Duchess
also joined the King on his journey to Avignon,
where they were met by Richelieu, newly made

---

[1] The loss of the Duc de Fronsac was especially to be deplored, since
he was a mere boy of twenty, and had arrived at Montpellier on the
previous day for his first campaign.

[2] Du Cros, 66–8.

Cardinal. From Avignon Montmorency returned
to Beaucaire for the meeting of the Estates and
then proceeded to Paris, arriving about the same
time as his wife who had journeyed there by
slower stages with the Court.

CHAPTER V

The Montmorencys in Paris—The Duke as patron of
literature—His reputed lack of wit—Quarrel with
Bassompierre — Théophile de Viau — Other poets
patronized by Montmorency—Jean Mairet—Quarrel
between the families of Montmorency and Lorraine—
The Duke recalled from Languedoc—Soubise captures
the royal fleet—Montmorency as Admiral sets off for
Brittany—His adventurous voyage in search of the
Dutch fleet—He persuades Admiral Haultain to sail
against La Rochelle—He wins the confidence of the
Dutch—Van Dorp refuses to sail—A preliminary brush
with the Rochellais—Death of Gadancour—Why the
English contingent was delayed—Montmorency defeats
Soubise's fleet—Capture of Ré—Montmorency's scrupulous regard for the terms of the capitulation—The King's
delight—Montmorency's cold reception at Court—He is
ordered to negotiate a truce with La Rochelle—He
narrowly escapes drowning—He represents the King at
the christening of Condé's son—He rejoins his wife at
Beaucaire—Her anxiety during his absence and conse-
quent illness—His presence restores her to health.

The Duc and Duchesse de Montmorency, who
for once were basking in the sun of royal favour,
now remained away from Languedoc for more
than a year, dividing their time between their
house in Paris and the Château of Chantilly. In
Paris they occupied the Hôtel neuf de Montmorency in the Rue St Avoie, a magnificent Renaissance
building designed by Pierre Lescot. Its famous

great gallery designed by Nicolo de Modena and decorated by Primaticcio contained an almost priceless collection of works of art, the greater part of which had been amassed by the Duke's grandfather, the Constable Anne de Montmorency.

Both in Paris and at Chantilly the Duke and Duchess gathered around them a galaxy of writers and poets. Both of them professed an interest in literature, although their tastes in this respect were far from being similar. Montmorency preferred poetry and romances to the more serious works affected by Marie Félice, who would regale herself with Seneca and the ancients. Her answer to her husband when he tried to persuade her to read his favourite literature is very charming: "I perceive more fine deeds in your own life than in your romances."[1]

Montmorency does not appear to have tried his own hand at writing, the sole piece attributed to him being an agreeable if somewhat feeble conceit in verse in the form of an epigram on the coat of arms of his wife's family.[2]

> La rose et le serpent d'Ursine
> Sont d'un naturel si bénin
> Que la rose n'a point d'épine
> Et le serpent point de venin.

But if Montmorency possessed no literary talent himself he at least knew how to appreciate

<hr>

[1] Monlaur, 74.   [2] Quoted by Rénée, 34 and Monlaur, 145.

talent in others. He showed ready patronage
to poets and, what was more unusual, was always
willing to submit to their judgment in literary
matters. He himself did not possess that reputation for wit so coveted in this age of polite
conversation. In *Le Grand Cyrus* Mademoiselle
de Scudéri says that his wit was commonplace:—
'he pleased rather by an inexplicable charm which
was in all his actions and all his person than by
the things which he said.' In the opinion of
Tallemant des Réaux, while he was not actually
a fool he was not quick-witted. The same
authority relates that as he found some difficulty
in expressing himself and was inclined to get
involved in his speech he was wont to help himself
out with gestures. But in spite of these dis-
advantages somehow he seemed to charm all who
met him. The Duc de Candale once watched the
throng at Court crowding round him and making
much of him, although to all appearance he had
done nothing but gesticulate. Candale turned to
his neighbour and remarked: "How lucky it is that
that man has got arms."[1]

Bassompierre, who was always inclined to be
jealous of Montmorency, was used to exercize his
mordant wit on him, but it must be admitted
that if he could not best him Montmorency did
at least sometimes come off creditably in the

[1] Tallemant des Réaux.

encounter.[1] On one occasion Bassompierre, who was not a good dancer, thought he saw Montmorency poking fun at his clumsy efforts and angrily said to him, "It is true that you are nimbler with your feet than I, but I am nimbler in other respects than you." To this Montmorency replied: "If I have not so sharp a tongue as you, I will show you I have as sharp a sword." "Yes," laughed Bassompierre, "you have that of the great Âne de Montmorency."[2] This interchange of pleasantries might have led to serious consequences, had not the friends of both parties intervened.

Montmorency's conversational gifts may not have been up to the high standard of the Court, but with his soldiers and his dependents the manner mattered more than the actual words and he did manage to impress them with the conviction that he had the happy knack of saying exactly the right thing to them. It was this strange charm of his quite as much as his bravery and generosity that won him the hearts of the soldiery.

Scudéri, who dedicated his first romance to Montmorency, calls him 'the father of the soldiers

---

[1] Bassompierre (II, 133) speaks of a quarrel with Montmorency in November, 1617, though he does not give any details. This particular incident appears to have occurred at one of the balls held before Lent in February, 1620. Bassompierre himself (II, 147) styles it a trifling dispute which was speedily settled.

[2] Tallemant des Réaux.

and the protector of the poets.' The praise was deserved. The Duke's care and thoughtfulness for his troops in time of war was equalled in time of peace by his generosity and kindness to struggling writers. He used to provide them with pensions and lodge them at his own house.[1] One of his favourites was Théophile de Viau, a poet of Huguenot origin. Montmorency introduced him to Court, where he attracted the favourable notice of Louis XIII. Unfortunately he possessed a somewhat lascivious Muse, and in 1619 the King, displeased at the profanity and licentiousness of his verse, banished him from Court and ordered Montmorency to dismiss him. After two years of exile he was forgiven and recalled, doubtless through the good offices of Montmorency, whom he accompanied in his campaign against the Protestants in 1622 and 1623. But presently there appeared a book called *La Parnasse Satyrique* which contained certain scandalous verses attributed by the editor to Théophile. Whether he really wrote them or not is uncertain; he himself strenuously denied their authorship, declaring that he had become reformed under the gentle influence of the Duchesse de Montmorency. Nevertheless, the Jesuits, always careful guardians of morality, demanded his trial, and he was found guilty by the Parlement and condemned to be burnt alive.

[1] Preface to Mairet's *La Sylvie.*

They had to content themselves, however, with burning him in effigy, for Montmorency contrived to spirit him away and keep him concealed in a turret at Chantilly.[1] While in hiding he occupied himself in writing verse addressed to his protector and to the Duchess, whom he invoked under the name of Sylvie because of her love for the woods with which the Château was surrounded. He was foolish enough to emerge from concealment too soon, and was at once discovered and thrown into prison. His sentence would now have been carried out, had not Montmorency insistently interceded for him and persuaded others to do so, including the all-powerful English ambassador, the Duke of Buckingham.[2] After being kept in prison for some time and subjected to endless interrogatories he was eventually released in September, 1625. He died in 1626 at the Hôtel de Montmorency, having been pardoned by the King and allowed to return to Paris shortly before.

Other poets who enjoyed the generous patronage of Montmorency were Du Bail, who drew him under the name of Céliman in his romance *Selisandre*, Pierre de Boissat, a writer of elegant Latin verse, and the dramatist Jean Mairet, a disciple of Théophile, and author of *Sophonisbe*, generally accounted the finest play in the French

---

[1] Théophile, *La Maison de Sylvie*.
[2] Rénée, 50; *Mercure*, 1625, XI, 1013-35.

PLATE III

CHANTILLY

LELEVATION DV BASTIMENT
ELEVATIO ÆDIFICII

[face p. 86

language before Corneille. His pastoral play *La Sylvie* was dedicated to the Duke, while to Marie Félice he dedicated *La Silvanire*, which he described as the younger sister of his former work. The Duke appointed him his secretary in 1625, and, like Théophile, he went on campaign, showing great bravery and celebrating the heroic exploits of his patron in flamboyant verse. In gentler vein he wrote many a poem to the Duchess, whom he also addressed as Sylvie. For her he celebrated the delights of Chantilly and composed laments on the Duke's absence when he was away at the wars.

The years between the autumn of 1622 and the early summer of 1625 seem to have been the happiest and most peaceful in Montmorency's life. His biographer, Du Cros, throws no light on his doings at this time, nor is Désormeaux more enlightening. All that can be ascertained is that he divided his time between the Court and Chantilly with occasional visits to his government of Languedoc to see that all was well there. Almost the only incident that emerges was a serious quarrel between the families of Montmorency and Lorraine in the autumn of 1623.[1] At the time of the King's marriage the Constabless de Montmorency, stepmother of the Duke, had been appointed Lady of Honour to the Queen, it being understood that no

[1] Bassompierre, III, 181.

one else was ever to be placed over her. But now the Duchesse de Chevreuse[1] was made superintendent of the Queen's household with precedence over all the other ladies. The Constabless was highly indignant and threatened to resign her post. Montmorency at once warmly espoused the cause of his father's widow. Feeling ran very high in the matter until at last Louis XIII himself, for once living up to his surname of 'the Just', solved the problem in the only possible manner by requesting both ladies to resign and giving both exactly the same compensation for the loss of their posts.[2]

Except for domestic troubles of this nature this had been a time of comparative peace for the warlike Montmorency, but beneath the apparent calm the Protestant whirlpool was seething, and the Duke was soon to have further opportunities of engaging in his favourite pastime. In May, 1625, he was suddenly recalled to Paris from Languedoc, where he had gone to hold the Estates at Béziers. He set off post-haste, leaving the Maréchal de Thémines to take his place in command of the forces in Languedoc.[3]

The situation with which he was called in to deal was one of acute seriousness. The Protes-

---

[1] Marie de Rohan Montbazon, married 1st, the Duc de Luynes, and 2nd, Claude de Lorraine, Duc de Chevreuse.
[2] Monlaur, 123.
[3] *Mercure,* 1625, XI, 747; Desormeaux, 234.

tant leaders, Rohan and Soubise, had recently
strengthened themselves by an alliance with Spain,
and in February, 1625, Soubise, determined to
safeguard La Rochelle by anticipating any possible attack on it, had performed the Drake-like
exploit of sailing suddenly into Port Blavel and
capturing the entire royal fleet. Since the Protestants had enlisted the aid of a Catholic power,
Richelieu, who was now at the head of affairs,
subtly decided to adjust the balance of power by
calling in the Protestant powers against their
co-religionists. Accordingly he made arrangements to hire Dutch and English ships and with
these proposed to gain possession of the islands of
Ré and Oléron as a preliminary to an attack on La
Rochelle itself.

Montmorency had been recalled in order that
in his capacity of Grand Admiral he might take
command of the French fleet. The facts that
the fleet was at this time non-existent, that there
was not one single ship on which he could even
fly his standard, and that his request for one had
of necessity to be refused, did not appear to dis-
turb the authorities.[1] In the circumstances it
would not have been surprising if he had displayed
a reluctance to go, as Richelieu says he did.[2] Du
Cros on the other hand declares that he was eager
to go in spite of the remonstrances of his friends,

[1] Desormeaux, 238.   [2] Richelieu, *Mémoires* (Lair), V, 50.

who pertinently enquired what he hoped to accomplish without either ships or money. But whether it was with ardour or reluctance at all events he set forth.

On his journey to Brittany he was accompanied by several friends who had volunteered to join him. Amongst them were the Marquis de Bressieux, the Comte de Vauvert, and his old-time enemy, the Duc de Retz. His kinsman Montmorency-Bouteville followed him in his capacity of Vice-Admiral. At Saumur the Duke received the news that the Dutch fleet had recently got the worst of it and had one ship burnt and five captured in a skirmish with Soubise. It appears that the Huguenots had beguiled the Dutch admiral, Haultain,[1] with fair words, assuring him that they were reluctant to fight against their co-religionists and that they were relieved to think that they would not be forced to do so, since they had heard that peace had been concluded and were momentarily expecting the confirmation of this intelligence. Thus they had lulled him into a false sense of security before setting upon him. Montmorency was not altogether displeased to hear this news, for he thought that the indignation of the Dutch at this piece of treachery might lighten

---

[1] The Dutch admiral's name is variously given by French writers as Houstein, Houstain, Haustain, Haustsain, and Haultain. The last is right. He was a member of the family of Soete or Zoete, Heeren van Haultain (A. J. van Aa, *Biographisch Woordenboek der Nederlanden*).

his task of persuading them to attack their professed friends.[1]

At Nantes he met the Duc de Vendôme who assured him with true candour that he was quite mad to set off utterly unprepared in this manner. Montmorency proudly answered that he found nothing impossible if it was for the King's service, that if was not the first time he had made war in conditions of extreme difficulty, and that he was resolved to face the hazards of the sea, though he knew full well that they surpassed all others.[2]

When he arrived at Sables d'Olonne he heard that the Dutch were refitting at Morbian and that after their recent defeat they seemed more inclined to return home than to proceed against La Rochelle.[3] Montmorency realized that at all costs their desertion must be prevented immediately. He despatched a messenger to the Dutch admiral who returned the disconcerting answer that he had not received orders to act against his conscience and that he would far rather fight with the Rochellais than against them.[4] On receiving this reply Montmorency decided that this was clearly an occasion for the exercize of his personal influence. With a few companions, including Bressieux, Soudeilles, a lieutenant in his Guards, and five or six servants, he boarded a small

[1] Du Cros, 76; *Mercure*, 1625, XI, 874.   [3] Du Cros, 79.
[2] Du Cros, 78; Desormeaux, 240.   [4] Desormeaux, 241.

fishing-boat and set out in search of the Dutch
fleet.[1]

It was an adventurous voyage. For three days
the little vessel was tossed about by a severe
storm to say nothing of being pursued by a
marauding corsair. On the fourth day they
sighted a ship coming from the direction of Morbian, and when it came nearer Montmorency caused
it to be hailed. The sailors of the strange vessel
appeared from their clothes to be French, but,
says Du Cros, they spoke a language that no one
could understand, though in the end it transpired
that it was Breton. Communications were eventually established by signs, and Montmorency learnt
from them that the Dutch fleet was still on the
high seas. This was discouraging news for the Duke
who had imagined that the fleet was at Morbian.
He decided to send out three small fishing-boats
in different directions to continue the search while
he himself awaited their report at Ny.[2]

On the following day he received news that
the Dutch had arrived at Isle Dieu and at once
proceeded to join their fleet. The story of his
intrepid voyage fortunately prepossessed the
gallant Dutch admiral in the Duke's favour. He
was impressed, astonished, and a trifle ashamed
and begged Montmorency to have a little more
care for his own safety in future.

[1] Du Cros, 79.   [2] Du Cros, 80–1.

Montmorency had no easy task in persuading
Haultain to proceed against La Rochelle, and it
is, in truth, amazing that he succeeded. He
flattered and cajoled him, appealed to his pride
to avenge his recent defeat by Soubise, insinuated
that his very honour as a soldier was at stake,
and assured him that he need have no scruples of
conscience, since the King's quarrel with the
Rochellais was not that they were Huguenots
but that they were rebels. But once he had been
convinced no one could have been a more faithful
friend and ally than Haultain.[1] He gave Montmorency his loyal support when it came to the
point of calling a council of the Dutch captains
and winning them over as well. In this also
Montmorency proved successful, chiefly by the
exercize of his great personal charm and his
princely gift of showing a personal interest in
every individual.

It was out of the question to proceed at once
against La Rochelle partly because the winds
were persistently contrary and partly also because
the expected English contingent had not yet
arrived. The problem was how to keep the Dutch
in good humour during the forced period of delay.
Montmorency could not help reflecting that the
winds unfavourable for the voyage to La Rochelle
were exceedingly favourable for the voyage to

[1] *Ibid*, 83.

Holland. He found the right solution in pandering to the notorious weakness of the Dutch for the pleasures of the table. He plied them so generously with food and drink that they no longer displayed any desire to be gone.[1] He also won their hearts by taking tobacco with them—a habit which in secret he utterly detested.[2]

In the meantime Montmorency sent Bressieux and the other companions of his voyage to await his return at Sables d'Olonne. As was his wont he did not hesitate to expend large sums of his own money and provided a table at his own charges for the eighty volunteers who had come to take part in the expedition.[3] He himself did not dare to leave the Dutch, but remained on Haultain's flagship all the time save for one brief visit to dry land.

Presently news came that the English contingent was on its way and had reached Dieppe, and about the same time Bouteville and Bressieux came to inform him that the fireships and armed chaloupes he had ordered to be prepared were ready.[4] On receipt of this news Montmorency decided to set sail for Ré, his plan being to capture this island and defeat the Rochellais fleet before attempting to lay siege to the city of La Rochelle itself.

[1] Du Cros, 81.   [3] Du Cros, 83; Desormeaux, 262.
[2] Desormeaux, 243; Pitaval, 70. [4] Du Cros, 85.

At the very last moment the Dutch vice-admiral, Van Dorp,[1] demurred and refused to sail, asserting that he had come there not to fight but to make peace. Montmorency was particularly annoyed that opposition should come from this man, since he had been at pains to provide him with a new ship, that which he had formerly commanded having been lost in the skirmish with Soubise. Haultain, between whom and Van Dorp no love was lost, was anxious to court-martial him for insubordination, but Montmorency preferred a quicker method. He signalled to the vice-admiral that if he did not weigh anchor after three warnings from a cannon he would sink his ship. The hint proved sufficient, and the recalcitrant Van Dorp sailed with the rest.[2]

The first attempt on Ré was abortive. It had been intended that the troops, commanded by the Duc de la Rochefoucauld, the Comte de St Luc, and Toiras, should make a descent on the island under cover of the fleet; but shortly after they had embarked on board the transports a storm sprang up and they were forced to land again. Meanwhile Montmorency with the fleet put out to sea owing to the dangers of the coast in such weather. The storm lasted for several days. The delay was not altogether inconvenient to Montmorency himself, since

---

[1] Admiral Filips van Dorp. In French books his name also is variously spelt: Urb, Durpe, Dorpt, Bruch, etc.

[2] Du Cros, 85; Desormeaux, 244.

it gave him ample opportunities to strengthen the hold he had already gained over the sailors. Their growing admiration for him was increased by his cool indifference to danger and by the ready way in which he adapted himself to the rigours of a life to which he had not been used.

It was at this time that Montmorency received letters from the Court commanding him not to engage with the enemy before the arrival of the English contingent unless he could feel absolutely certain of victory. In view of this communication the Council of War decided that it would be wiser and safer to wait for the reinforcements which they knew were on the way.[1]

A preliminary brush with the Rochellais occurred when one of their scouting-vessels came out and was attacked by three of Montmorency's armed chaloupes under Gadancour, the Captain of his Guards, and the Chevalier de Cangey. There ensued a brave skirmish in the course of which all the combatants were pretty well knocked to pieces before night fell and ended the business. Gadancour, who had fought bravely all day and had almost miraculously escaped without a scratch, was unfortunately slain by the very last cannon-ball that was fired in the engagement. Montmorency was deeply grieved at the loss of this gallant gentleman; but he was fortunate in being able to fill his place

[1] Du Cros, 86.

with one no less brave and devoted, Soudeilles, who remained with him to the end of his career.[1]

Partly because of the bad weather and partly because of the orders from Court Montmorency returned to Isle Dieu until, on September the 12th, news came that the English contingent was at hand. The reasons for its long delay are well worth recording. As a condition of the marriage-treaty between the Prince of Wales and Henrietta Maria of France James I had agreed that he would lend Louis XIII one man of war and would allow seven English merchant-ships to be hired of their owners. It was understood that they were to be used against the King of Spain and his Italian allies, and a special provision was made that they were not to be employed against the French Protestants. But there being some suspicion that this condition might not be observed James stipulated that the greater part of the crews were to be Englishmen.

In pursuance of this arrangement Captain John Pennington proceeded to France with a squadron consisting of His Majesty's ship *Vanguard* and seven privately-owned vessels. Having heard, however, that the French designed to send him against La Rochelle and that they had also hired a Dutch fleet for that purpose, he sent a hasty despatch to the Lord High Admiral, the Duke of Buckingham,

[1] Du Cros, 86–8.

H

declining to continue the service and requesting his immediate recall. To his astonishment and dismay he received the reply that he was to execute his orders and hand his ships over to the French, but that he himself was not to relinquish command over them. This message was handed to him at Dieppe by the French Ambassador, who also brought him a letter from Louis XIII requiring him to receive his admiral, the Duc de Montmorency, and his army and to proceed against the rebels at La Rochelle. This Pennington flatly refused to do in spite of all remonstrances, threats, and protests. His own men backed him up and insisted upon sailing immediately for England, declaring stoutly that they would rather be hanged at home than be slaves to the French and fight against the Protestant religion.

As soon as the squadron had anchored in the Downs Pennington sent to Buckingham to inform him of what had happened and assured him on behalf of the seamen that they would rather die than return to France. But the King and his council had received no official intimation of the projected expedition against La Rochelle—although it appears that they did receive private intimation of it from the Duc de Rohan—and it was decided that no reasonable justification could be found for breaking His Majesty's solemn engagement with the King of France. Strict orders were sent to

Pennington to return at once to France and to place his ship in the hands of the Marquis D'Effiat. The seven merchant-ships were likewise to put themselves into the service of France. Pennington now had no other alternative than to sail back to France and surrender his ship. At the last moment the crews of the other vessels refused to obey the ignominious order and endeavoured to make their escape back to England. Pennington was obliged to arrest their flight by firing at them, and they all returned to Dieppe with the exception of the *Neptune*, whose captain, Sir Ferdinando Gorges, a veteran who had sailed the seas in Elizabeth's days and had accompanied Essex on the Island Voyage, succeeded in bringing her away. But though the ships had to be handed over, their crews resolutely refused to serve in them and, following Pennington's own example, they all, with the exception of one gunner, quitted their ships and returned to England.[1] When they joined Montmorency the ships of the English contingent were manned entirely by French crews, save, of course, for the nameless gunner.[2]

On Sunday, September the 14th, the English ships arrived at last and at eleven o'clock that evening the fleet set sail for Ré. When it arrived off the island at five o'clock the next morning

---

[1] Echard's *History of England*, 1720, p. 422.
[2] Richelieu, *Mémoires*, (Lair), V, 57.

Montmorency was informed that Soubise's fleet was lying up in the mouth of the river Laye. He was unable to seek out the enemy before midday as he had to wait for the tide. When the two fleets at last came into contact there began a furious cannonade which lasted until five o'clock in the afternoon. Montmorency was delighted that the Dutch Government had ordered their admiral to lead the vanguard, since he himself, being on the flagship, was in the forefront of the battle as he ever wished to be.[1] Although he had no ship of his own, as Grand Admiral of France he was commander-in-chief of the allied fleet and was actually in charge of the operations. His bold attack on Soubise's fleet of 26 ships and the masterly manner in which he handled it in spite of his inexperience of sea-warfare amazed and delighted the Dutch. The enemy fleet fled before him and retired far up the creek, where, when the tide receded, several of their ships ran aground.

Montmorency was now able to turn his attention to covering the descent of the landing-forces on the island of Ré. After two days of fierce fighting the whole of the island was occupied. Since the enemy fleet was apparently safely bottled up in the mouth of the Laye it was considered that no further danger was to be apprehended from that quarter and that

[1] Du Cros, 89; Bassompierre, III, 210.

the best course for the royal fleet was to lie between
Ré and La Rochelle to prevent any help being sent
to the defenders of the island. But suddenly the
wind veered round and a portion of the Rochellais
fleet under Guiton was enabled to get out of the
creek and make an unexpected reappearance. The
Dutch were reluctant to engage again and were in
favour of drawing off, especially as a considerable
portion of the troops on board had been landed to
help in Ré; but Montmorency insisted, and all
those on board the flagship were bidden to brandish
their naked swords aloft as a signal for the attack.
The victory was complete; the Rochellais fleet
fled and was pursued by the Royal fleet all night.
In the morning it was found that eight enemy
vessels had been captured and most of the rest
either burnt or sunk.[1]

Since the fleet had been dispersed or destroyed
and Ré had been taken, the defenders of Oléron
decided that it would be futile to offer any resistance, and so a few days later surrendered to Montmorency without a blow.

Under the terms of the capitulation accorded
to the defenders of Ré by Montmorency on September the 18th there was to be an immediate
armistice. The soldiers of the garrison were to
retain their lives and liberty and were to be con-

---

[1] The account of the naval operations is based mainly on *Mercure*,
1625, XI, 877–888.

voyed to La Rochelle in safety on the sole condition that they would undertake not to bear arms against the King again for six months.[1] Montmorency himself supervised the transportation in order to make sure that his promises were faithfully carried out. Du Cros relates that so scrupulous was the Duke as to keeping such an agreement to the very letter that those who had charge of the arrangements for convoying the surrendered garrisons to La Rochelle were so fearful of infringing his strict orders in the least particular that when the wind carried away a soldier's hat into the water they actually sent a fishing-boat out to fetch it.[2] Whether absolutely true or not, this is typical of the stories told of Montmorency and reveals what was thought of him by the soldiery whether they were fighting under him or against him. To them he was a man whose very lightest word could be trusted implicitly. On this occasion he showed the utmost generosity to the large number of those who had surrendered at Ré who turned out to be natives of Languedoc. All these men he sent for, and, after making them promise not to bear arms against the King again, he gave each one of them enough money to enable him to return to his home.[3] His magnanimity and courtesy to a defeated enemy so impressed the citizens of La

[1] *Mercure*, 1625, XI, 889–890; Du Cros, 99.
[2] Du Cros, 105.   [3] Pitaval, 78.

Rochelle that they sent a special deputation from the city to offer him their thanks.[1]

The victory was celebrated by processions and salvoes of artillery. Montmorency's praises were sung on all sides and celebrated in verse by Mairet, who himself had been present at the battle and had acquitted himself gallantly. Montmorency received an enthusiastic letter of thanks and congratulation from the King, who appears on this occasion to have been really delighted and for several days would speak of nothing else but Montmorency's courage. He also received the signal honour of a personal letter of congratulation from the Pope, Urban VII. Nevertheless, so powerful were the jealous influences at work against him that when he arrived at the Court at St. Germain he met with a very frigid reception. He had thought that in a personal interview with the King he might be able to put forward his views regarding the advisability of an early attack on La Rochelle, which, blockaded by the fleet and deprived of the two islands that formed its best defences, was in an exposed condition. He offered to advance the expense if he were placed in command and declared himself willing to stake all his fortune and reputation on the success of the venture.[2] He announced that he had come to Court because he was under the impression that

[1] *Ibid.*   [2] Desormeaux, 263.

he could best serve the King's interests at the
moment by being with him to give him counsel on
a matter about which he had quite exceptional
knowledge. But Louis XIII disagreed with him
entirely as to the desirability of his presence at
Court and told him curtly that his place was with
the fleet. There can be little doubt that his
refusal to listen to Montmorency's scheme was
inspired by Cardinal Richelieu, who was unwilling
that Montmorency should receive the credit for
the successful accomplishment of so important an
undertaking. He was ordered to return at once
to the fleet and start negotiations for a truce with
La Rochelle.

His return was delayed for a few days by a
mysterious fever which he himself appears to have
thought resulted from a deliberate attempt to
poison him. He was obliged to halt for several
days at Bourges. When he rejoined the fleet he
found Admiral Haultain about to return to Holland. The Dutch admiral had conceived a very
great affection for him, liking him for his gaiety,
charm, and generosity, and admiring him for his
valour and enterprise. His genuine affection was
increased, says Du Cros, by the fact that Montmorency had persuaded the King of France to
confer on him the Order of St. Michael, which he
had greatly coveted.[1]

[1] Du Cros, 112.

The time Montmorency spent with the fleet while awaiting the King's instructions to treat for peace with La Rochelle was not devoid of adventure. On one occasion he narrowly escaped being captured by the enemy, and on another he was nearly drowned. One day the Maréchal de Thémines had been dining on board ship with him. When the party broke up to go ashore, the sea was so rough that it was thought inadvisable to use the ordinary light boat, and a heavier one was brought alongside. There was only room for one of them in it, so Montmorency, leaving it for his guest, himself leapt into the merest cockleshell of a skiff. Great were his horror and consternation when the Maréchal, as heavy in politeness as he was in body, suddenly descended into his frail vessel and refused to leave it, although it was very nearly sinking beneath their combined weights and that of the one sailor who was to row it. But to the relief of the crowd of horrified, anxious, and helpless onlookers they eventually managed to reach dry land without mishap. [1]

Montmorency was the ideal intermediary for effecting peace between the King and La Rochelle, and he discharged the duty swiftly, admirably, and apparently to the satisfaction of both parties. Immediately the task was accomplished he proceeded to Bourges to represent the King at the

[1] Du Cros, 128.

christening of his own nephew, the Duc d'Enghien, son of his sister, the Princesse de Condé. The ceremony took place on May the 6th, 1626.[1]

As soon as he was free he hastened to Beaucaire where his wife was then staying. Her anxiety for his safety when he was at the wars was always very great, but during the naval campaign it had been so intense and so abnormal that she had made herself seriously ill. Her constitution was by no means robust in the first place and she tried it sorely by the rigorous penances and privations to which she subjected herself.[2] This habit, coupled with her anxiety, reduced her to such a state that she lay on her bed in a sort of languor, refusing both food and drink, scarcely uttering a word save to murmur to herself over and over again: "If I were to lose him!"[3] By the time her husband returned she had become so weak that the doctors warned him she would inevitably die unless she could be persuaded to take some nourishment. With lover-like intuition Montmorency found the means to coax her. He dressed himself in the garb affected by the local fishermen and thus arrayed went to her apartment and told her that he wanted to go fishing, but that he refused to give himself this pleasure until she had promised to eat everything he caught. This

Du Cros, 133; *Mercure*, 1626, XII, 305.   [1] Cotolendi. 35.
[2] Rénée, 73.

was the sort of cajolement which Marie Félice always found it impossible to resist.[1]

The Duke's eager attentions together with her pride in the glory with which his return to her had been invested contributed more than anything else to her recovery, and, when she was a little stronger, Montmorency on Ranchin's advice took her to drink the waters at Balaruc, where she became entirely restored to health.

[1] *Ibid.*, 74; Monlaur, 131

CHAPTER VI

Richelieu suspicious of Montmorency—Ornano's conspiracy—Chalais implicates Montmorency—Richelieu persuades Montmorency to resign his office of Admiral in the hope of being made Constable—The Duke's resentment at the Cardinal's duplicity—The Montmorencys in Languedoc—Bouteville's duel with Beuvron—His flight and capture—Richelieu decides on his execution—The nobles intercede for him—Montmorency's letter to the King—Last appeals by Bouteville's womenfolk—Execution of Bouteville and Des Chapelles—Montmorency's resentment—Louis XIII's attempts to conciliate him—Rohan makes advances to Montmorency—Rebellion of Rohan—Montmorency takes measures against him—The Battle of Souilles—Montmorency's promptness goes unrewarded—Condé appointed commander-in-chief—Condé and Montmorency at Toulouse—Capture of Pâmiers—Condé orders Montmorency to advance on Nimes—Montmorency's letter to Condé—He ravages the surroundings of Nimes—Capture of Gallargues—Montmorency's grief at the fate of the prisoners—Quarrel with Bassompierre—Siege of Privas—Death of the Marquis de Portes—Siege of Alais—Montmorency injured by a flying stone—The King deprecates his rashness—Negotiations for peace—The Édit des Élus—Montmorency persuades the Estates of Languedoc to accept it—Richelieu entertained by the Montmorencys at La Grange.

On his return to Paris Montmorency was deeply chagrined at the coldness of his reception at Court. More especially was he both amazed and

indignant that all the credit of his recent exploit
should now have been given to Toiras, to whom
also was granted the governorship of the island
of Ré, for which he himself had asked. The fact
of the matter was that, rightly or wrongly, Montmorency was regarded with deep suspicion by
Richelieu. At the beginning of the year 1626
there was much talk of a movement at Court to
procure the entry of the King's brother, Gaston,
into the Council in order to counteract the overwhelming influence of the Cardinal. Louis XIII's
health was far from good; although he had been
long married he had as yet no child, and Gaston
was the heir presumptive. The prime movers in
this plan, the exact objects of which have never
been fathomed, were Gaston's Governor, the
Maréchal d'Ornano, and the intriguing Duchesse
de Chevreuse; but many others of the great
nobles were more or less involved, including Condé,
Soissons, Angoulême, Montmorency, Schomberg,
Lesdiguières, and Longueville. It is unlikely,
indeed, that there was any truth in the rumour
that there was a sinister and deep-laid plot to
supplant Louis by Gaston and to marry the new
King to Anne of Austria. The absurdity of such
an idea was succinctly expressed by the Queen
herself when she declared that she would not have
gained enough by the change! But there is no
doubt that it was intended to break the power

of the Cardinal, and there was overt opposition
to his plan to marry Gaston to Mademoiselle de
Montpensier. Richelieu believed—and doubtless
with reason—that Montmorency was among those
who would willingly have upset the project of the
Montpensier marriage and married Gaston to
Condé's daughter.

Whatever their hopes and plans may have been,
at any rate the Cardinal was too strong for his
opponents. Ornano was seized and imprisoned,
the Duchesse de Chevreuse was banished, and the
Cardinal himself officiated at the marriage of
Gaston to Mademoiselle de Montpensier. Richelieu
did not attempt to take any measures against the
others, possibly because they were too numerous
and too powerful and possibly also because their
projects, however distasteful they may have been
to him, could not exactly be characterized as
plotting. The sole victim was the Comte de
Chalais, who was condemned by a special com-
mission and executed. During his interrogatories
Chalais implicated many others, including Montmorency, who, he asserted, had been brought
into the plan by women. 'He had so much
inclination for the ladies and was so ruled by them
that whenever they had some discontent and
wished to make use of him, he was prepared to
obey them in everything. This being the case,
there is no doubt that they would form a union

between Monsieur and Monsieur le Prince and Montmorency.'[1]

How much there was in these intrigues it is difficult to say. Desormeaux denies that Montmorency took any part in them,[2] but, even supposing that he did, the question then arises as to how far his part in them could be considered culpable and how far as perfectly legitimate political action. It is, indeed, far from unlikely that, considering the Cardinal's treatment of him, Montmorency should have adhered to the party that was opposed to him and should have joined in any schemes to counteract his influence by legitimate methods. In his memoirs Richelieu states that three years later Condé admitted to him that after Gaston had married Mademoiselle de Montpensier Montmorency had endeavoured to persuade him, Condé, to marry his daughter to the Comte de Soissons, thus uniting many interests and bringing himself, Soissons, Longueville, and Monsieur together in a party hostile to the Cardinal. Condé also told him that Montmorency had repeatedly warned him that the Cardinal was intriguing against him.[3]

Montmorency certainly had many causes of feeling aggrieved against the Cardinal. Another disappointment came to him in the autumn of

---

[1] Richelieu. *Mémoires* (Lair), VI, 113–114.   [2] Desormeaux, 266.
[3] Richelieu, *Mémoires* (Mich et Pouj), VII, 593.

1626. The Constable Lesdiguières died in September of this year. Richelieu decided that this would be an excellent opportunity to suppress the office altogether and at the same time to extinguish the other great office of Grand Admiral, which was held by Montmorency. These charges in his opinion not only derogated from the pre-eminence of the royal power, but also introduced confusion into the national finances, since the Constable and Admiral had sole control over the war-chests and had been answerable to no one for their expenditure. While recognizing that these offices had been of great service to the State in days gone by, he maintained that they were now out of date and that Henri IV himself had acknowledged this fact and had only made Henri de Montmorency Constable because this was the sole means of withdrawing him with honour out of Languedoc, where his almost sovereign power might have been a menace to the Crown. These arguments were sound enough; it was the Cardinal's methods that were open to criticism. He persuaded Montmorency to lay down his office of Grand Admiral by cunningly extending to him the hope of becoming Constable, an office which he coveted more than anything else in the world, since it had so often been held by his ancestors.[1]   Richelieu, however, had no real

[1] Desormeaux, 265.

intention of allowing this post to be revived. He
was bent on crushing the power of the ancient
nobility and regarded these exalted offices as one
of the chief sources of their influence.

For resigning his office Montmorency received
1200,000 livres as compensation, 'a sum which,'
in Richelieu's own words, 'although it may seem
large, was not only very small, but was a great
gain to the King considering the glorious successes
of the following years which would never have
come to pass otherwise.'[1] From Montmorency's
point of view the sum was negligible; it was not
even sufficient to reimburse him for the enormous
expenses he had borne out of his own pocket in
the King's service during the naval campaign.[2]
Richelieu divested himself of all credit he might
have obtained for his action by virtually appointing
himself to the office vacated by Montmorency. He
took upon himself all the powers of the Grand
Admiral except that of actual command of the
fleet, though even in this respect the choice rested
with him. He assumed the title of '*Grand Maître
chef et surintendant général de la navigation et com-
merce de France.*'

Thoroughly upset by the way in which he had
been treated, Montmorency resolved to retire again
to Languedoc. Here he and the Duchess spent
the winter of 1626-7. The southern nobility

---

[1] Richelieu, *Mémoires* (Lair), VI, 294–8.   [2] Desormeaux, 266.

I

gathered around them at Béziers, and there they held their Court amid such gaiety as had not been since the beginning of the Civil troubles. A succession of festivities was held in their honour, the most notable being that offered to them by the officers of the Montpellier garrison on January the 31st, 1627. The ballet enacted on this occasion represented the building of the Tower of Babel. The Duke was complimented on the success of his recent naval campaign by the Parlement of Toulouse and other official bodies in a manner of honour never shown to any Governor before. At the opening of the Estates at Béziers a special resolution was passed thanking the Duchess for having supported the interests of the province with the King during her husband's absence.[1]

In the early summer of 1627 Montmorency became deeply concerned in the misfortunes of his kinsman, Louis de Montmorency, Comte de Bouteville, who was condemned to death for an offence against the duelling-edicts. It must be admitted that Bouteville's offence was flagrant. An inveterate duellist, he had fought no less than twenty-one duels. After the last of these encounters he had taken refuge in Brussels, but soon, tiring of exile, had besought Louis XIII to allow him to return in order that he might take part in the wars against the Protestants. The King

[1] Du Cros, 134; Monlaur, 138.

PLATE IV

ARMAND CARDINAL DE RICHELIEV DVC ET
Pair de France Grand M. Chef et Sur:Intendant de la
Navigation Gouuerneur, et Lieuten. gnal. pour le Roy au pais de Bretaigne.
A. Moncornet ex

[face p. 114

refused, but as a concession to the Archduchess Clara Eugenia of the Netherlands, who had supported his petition, he intimated that, if Bouteville chose to come back to France without official permission, he would not be pursued or molested so long as he did not enter Paris or approach the Court.[1] Bouteville was piqued by this refusal and defiantly resolved to return to Paris and openly fight the Marquis de Beuvron, with whom he had recently had a quarrel. The duel took place in the Place Royale on May the 12th, 1627, at midday, when the square was at its most frequented. As was the custom at that time the seconds also fought and there were three a side. One of Bouteville's supporters, his cousin and best friend, François de Rosmadec, Comte des Chapelles, killed his opponent, Bussy d'Amboise. Directly after the fight the survivors fled. Beuvron escaped to England in safety, but Bouteville and Des Chapelles were taken at Vitri-le-Brûlé near Méaux.[2]

In Richelieu's opinion it was high time that the edicts against duelling were enforced and he decided that an example should be made of Bouteville and Des Chapelles. In a memorandum on the subject which he sent to the King he pointed out that, although Bouteville's services had undoubtedly

[1] *Mercure*, 1627, XIII, 403.
[2] For the Bouteville incident see Du Cros, 135, *et seq.*; Richelieu, *Mémoires* (Lair), VII, 63–9; Desormeaux, 276.

been most valuable, his disregard of the edicts had positively become a habit. For six years owing to his quarrelsome disposition he had been at the bottom of most disputes of this kind at Court, and he showed no sign of mending his ways, but on the contrary promised to become a public danger. In truth, Bouteville seems to have been a difficult character. Duelling was a veritable passion with him. His very house was a sort of duelling-hell with a room specially fitted up as a school for duellists.[1] It was not that he was quick-tempered or choleric, he appears to have been just cold-bloodedly aggressive. So notorious was his reputation that the brave Marquis of Hamilton, speaking of him to D'Effiat, once remarked: "If that man sent me a challenge, I should not take it up, unless it was accompanied by a certificate from his doctor assuring me that his desire to fight was not due to some disease."

The Cardinal's decision not to pardon Bouteville and Des Chapelles caused a sensation all the more intense because the nobility had always regarded the duelling-edicts as not to be taken too seriously. Moreover, much interest was taken in Bouteville personally. He was of very illustrious lineage and closely allied to the great house of Montmorency, and he himself had led a useful military career, having taken a distinguished part in all the recent

[1] Pitaval, 97.

wars. At La Rochelle he had served under Montmorency as Vice-admiral. In view of these past
services many felt that this was an occasion when
the royal privilege of clemency might well be
exercized. Appeals were made for him by the
most exalted in the land, and the King was
petitioned on his behalf by his younger brother,
Gaston, the Queen-Mother, the Prince and Princesse
de Condé, the Duc d'Épernon, and Cardinal de la
Valette. Montmorency, who, besides being his
kinsman and his companion-in-arms, was personally much attached to him, sent several
messengers to intercede with the King and finally
wrote him the following letter.[1]

'Sire, if I had dared to leave this province without Your Majesty's permission I would have come
to throw myself at your feet and ask pardon for
my cousin de Bouteville . . . Sire, it is the
misfortune of the time, the distemper of those
of his age and humour more than any design to
displease Your Majesty, since he bears a name to
which fidelity and obedience are inseparably
attached. I believe that I may truthfully say this
and that I have some right to ask of Your Majesty
with all the submission that I owe to you the life
of this unhappy man in return for those of many

[1] *Lettres de Monseigneur le Prince de Condé. Ensemble celle de
Monseigneur de Montmorency, envoyée au Roy, sur le sujet du sieur de
Bouteville.* (A contemporary pamphlet). Also quoted by Du Cros,
135, and *Mercure*, 1627, XIII, 421–2.

of his ancestors and mine who lost them so gloriously in the service of their kings and for the welfare of your crown. Also if the services I have tried to render Your Majesty may merit some consideration, I venture to bring them to your memory to banish from it your justice and excite your pity. Sire, your pardon which your wisdom will know how to accompany with all the other punishments which his offence merits will without doubt make him wiser. I willingly make myself pledge for his obedience in the future, and as he has qualities which may make him useful to Your Majesty I firmly believe that the gratitude he will show in all his actions will give Your Majesty reason not to repent of having granted his life to one who bears the name of Montmorency.'

This eloquent and dignified appeal also fell on deaf ears. Urged thereto by Richelieu, Louis XIII remained inflexible. A last despairing effort was made by Bouteville's womenfolk. His wife, who was then expecting a child,[1] sent the King a long and pathetic appeal and persuaded the other illustrious ladies of the house of Montmorency to go with her to make a personal intercession. At first the King refused to see them, but in the end he acceded to the Duc d'Angoulême's urgent request and consented to receive them in the

[1] This child was later to become the famous Maréchal de Luxembourg.

Queen-Mother's apartments. The Comtesse de
Bouteville was accompanied by the Duchesse de
Montmorency[1] and the Duke's three sisters, the
Princesse de Condé, the Duchesse d'Angoulême,
and the Duchesse de Ventadour. They all threw
themselves on their knees at the King's feet in
tears and begged his mercy for the culprits. Louis
was visibly affected, especially when the Comtesse
de Bouteville swooned away at his feet, but he
persisted in his refusal to pardon either of the
delinquents, saying to the petitioners: "Their loss
touches me as much as you; but my conscience
forbids me to pardon them."[2]

Both Bouteville and Des Chapelles were
executed. There can be no question but that
their condemnation was perfectly legal and that
they deserved their fate. But Montmorency could
not help remarking that it was significant that
others had been pardoned for the same offence
and that when an example was made a member of
his own family should have been chosen. He
regarded Bouteville's execution as a blow deliberately aimed by Richelieu at his house, and he
was probably not far wrong in his estimate of
the Cardinal's motives. He made no attempt to
conceal his resentment, and Louis had some

---

[1] Marie Félice had evidently come to Paris alone. It is possible
that she had done so with the express purpose of pleading for Bouteville, since her husband was unable to leave Languedoc.

[2] Desormeaux, 290–1; *Mercure*, 1627, XIII, 450.

difficulty in pacifying him, though he took the trouble to write him a long personal letter and sent him a special messenger to explain the necessity for his action.[1] The King was no doubt relieved when at length he received a submissive letter from Montmorency intimating that his loyalty remained unaffected.[2] It was essential that he should not be alienated. There was renewed activity at La Rochelle and Montmorency's influence in the South was so considerable that it would have turned the scale had his resentment at his grievances induced him at this juncture to throw in his lot with the Huguenots. The danger that he might do so was far from being non-existent; since it was known that the Duc de Rohan had taken the opportunity of his dissatisfaction to endeavour to tempt him into rebellion, though there is no reason to believe that Montmorency ever responded to his advances.[3]

Having succeeded in making an alliance with the English, Rohan felt himself strong enough once more to take the offensive and in September, 1627, openly declared himself. His plan was to gather together an army of 20,000 men to rescue Montauban and then attack the royal army before La Rochelle. Montmorency was warned by spies of his military preparations and wrote to the

---

[1] *Mercure*, 1627, XIII, 422–3.   [2] *Ibid*, 424–5.
[3] Du Cros, 140.

Court reporting what he had heard and asking for
troops, money, and supplies. He received no
reply, and, deeming the matter of pressing importance, issued commissions on his own responsibility
and began to raise troops in Languedoc. That
he did not wait for orders from Court and thus
braved the royal displeasure disposes of Richelieu's
accusation that he was actually in sympathy
with Rohan and was forced to arm against his
will by the importunity of the Parlement of
Toulouse.[1] The silence of the Court would have
given him every excuse for inactivity. On the
contrary he put a spoke into Rohan's preparations
by stopping his levies, by sending St. Palais round
to the nobility of Languedoc to urge them to
remain loyal, and by persuading or bribing such
towns as Castre and Puylaurens to refuse Rohan
admittance. Then, as orders were still not forthcoming, he set out in pursuit of Rohan, who was
believed to be moving on Montauban. His own
troops were so few that he was advised not to
venture an attack. "Let me be," he said, "I will
attack them in a place where pistols and swords
will be more useful than muskets."[2] This remark
was characteristic of Montmorency's attitude towards war. He was a survival from the days
of knighthood when strength and valour counted
for everything. If hand-to-hand fighting had been

[1] Richelieu, *Mémoires* (Lair) VII, 236.   [2] Du Cros, 144.

all of war he would have been a great soldier, but
he was no strategist and certainly not a match
for Rohan or any other of the great generals of
his time. It was in the actual combat that he
shone, and his victories were gained not by subtle
manœuvres but by the sheer force of his attack.

Being an admirable strategist and possessing, as
he did, a consummate knowledge of the country,
Rohan was able to move his troops by devious
ways under cover of darkness, so that some time
elapsed before Montmorency could discover his
exact whereabouts. But at dawn on November
the 3rd his spies gave him the information he
needed, and he and the Duc de Ventadour set
forth hastily from St Félix de Caraman with their
cavalry and a small body of infantry they had
hastily collected together. They caught up with
Rohan at Souilles, near Castelnaudary, and Montmorency, in spite of his inferior numbers, decided
to force a battle on him.

During the fighting, which lasted for two hours,
Montmorency seemed to be everywhere at once,
dashing from one part of the line to another under
the enemy's fire, giving orders, and encouraging
his men. Rohan's losses were considerable and
eventually he thought it wiser to retreat. He
abandoned his dead and many of his wounded,
and Montmorency remained master of the field
of battle. It was not a really decisive victory,

since Rohan had had the good sense to draw off
before he was beaten; but there is no doubt that
Montmorency's prompt action compelled him to
change his plans. Instead of continuing his
advance on Montauban he made for the Comté
de Foix, where he was certain of being received
by the Huguenot towns. Montmorency was not
strong enough to carry the war into the enemy's
camp, but he succeeded in frustrating Rohan's
attempt to get to Montauban through Gascony
by causing all the boats to be destroyed at the
point where he proposed to cross the Garonne.[1]

Although Rohan's plans had been defeated by the
care and industry of Montmorency, the Duke's
action went unrewarded; he was not forgiven for
not awaiting orders from Court. When he sent
to get his commissions confirmed, his messenger,
St. Palais, was informed that such actions on the
part of anyone whose loyalty was less proven than
Montmorency's would have been regarded with
grave suspicion. "Your master," he was told,
"has undertaken in France without the consent of
the Court what the King of England cannot do
in his own realm without the consent of his parlia-
ment, having raised an army and granted commissions in France without the King's permission."[2]
The commissions were eventually confirmed, but
Montmorency was not put in command. The

---

[1] *Mercure*, 1627-8, XIV, 380-5.   [2] Pitaval, 106.

Prince de Condé was given supreme command of
the army. The choice of Condé was made because,
being a Prince of the Blood and the Duke's own
brother-in-law, he was one of the very few people
in the kingdom whom it was possible to place over
Montmorency in his own province. Richelieu
admits that the command should really have been
given to Montmorency himself as Governor of
Languedoc; but says that this was not done because
he was never very successful against Rohan 'either
through ill-luck or ill-management, or else because
he desired to keep in with the Huguenot faction
which his father had always protected and encouraged there.'[1] This calumnious insinuation
appears to have possessed no foundation. It
is said that the appointment of Condé was very
acceptable to Montmorency—Du Cros goes so far
as to assert that he actually requested it[2]—and it is
indeed probable that he was perfectly willing to
serve under his own brother-in-law. At any rate
he did his utmost to second him loyally and to
assist him in his inexperience.

On January the 15th, 1628, after reducing
several strongholds, Condé and Montmorency
entered Toulouse, where the Parlement solemnly
declared Rohan degraded from the peerage and
guilty of high treason and condemned him to be
torn in pieces by four horses. But the sentence

[1] Richelieu, *Mémoires* (Lair) VII, 246.   [2] Du Cros, 140.

could not be carried out except in effigy seeing that
Rohan, far from being a prisoner, was still at the
head of a large and powerful army. In the course
of the harangue which he delivered at the opening
of the Estates of Languedoc on March the 2nd
Condé paid ungrudging tribute to Montmorency's
capacity in the recent campaign. By way of
returning the compliment, on the same evening
Montmorency gave a sumptuous and costly ballet
in his brother-in-law's honour. It was remarked
that Condé did not appear to take much pleasure
in it and was asleep nearly all the time it was
being danced.[1]

While affecting to amuse himself at the Carnival
Montmorency was planning an attack on Pamiers.[2]
The siege, conducted by Montmorency and Condé
with an army of 4,000 men composed of volunteers
and raw levies, was begun on March the 4th and
lasted for ten days. On Palm Sunday Montmorency, in an attempt to drive Rohan out of the
Vivarais, set forth at the head of a small force
very inadequately supplied owing to the difficulty
of obtaining either food or money. The command,
says Du Cros, was honourable, but the means he was
given to execute it with were wholly insufficient.[3]

Although Rohan skilfully avoided a pitched
battle, Montmorency distinguished himself greatly

[1] *Mercure*, 1628, XIV, 72.   [2] Du Cros, 147.
[3] *Ibid*, 154.

on this campaign, invariably showing the most
amazing personal valour. Stronghold after stronghold fell before him. While waiting at Viviers
for help which he had sent for from Lyons and
Dauphiné to enable him to invest Pouzin he
decided to reduce Chomérac, which had revolted
from the King and was giving help to Pouzin and
Privas. On May the 20th he appeared before
Chomérac and, having summoned it in vain to
surrender, subjected it to a furious artillery fire
for twenty-four hours. The defenders then
expressed their willingness to give in, but Montmorency replied that it was now too late and
that he intended to take the place by storm. He
himself led the assault, leaping from rock to rock
like a mountain-goat. As this siege was in the
nature of a punitive expedition for contumacious
revolt Montmorency showed a sternness that
was uncommon in him. Those of the garrison
who survived were taken and hanged, the town
was burnt to ashes, and the castle demolished.[1]

On May the 25th he invested Pouzin which had
been newly fortified by Rohan. The place capitulated on June the 3rd. The Maréchal de Créqui
had deemed this fortress so strong that he had
asked Montmorency to send him a special messenger if he took it within a fortnight, and, when

---

[1] *Mercure,* 1628, XIV, 127; *Récit Véritable de la Reprise de Chaumeras,*
Bordeaux, 1628.

the news came of its fall after a week's siege,
declared that nothing could resist the fortune and
valour of Montmorency.[1]

Condé now commanded Montmorency to advance
upon Nîmes; but he declined to do so until the
reinforcements for which he had asked were
forthcoming. Condé was indignant, although he
had to confess that Montmorency was inadequately
supplied for such an undertaking. 'I have written
to M. de Montmorency three times to proceed
there,' he wrote to Richelieu, 'but, after the capture
of Pouzin, he went off to lay siege to Mirabel,
which he has just taken. He informs me by a
courier, who arrived yesterday, that he is proceeding to Valons: this is not on the way to Nîmes.
His reason is that he says he is too weak, and
certainly M. de Rohan is very strong in infantry,
and without forces much greater than mine or
M. de Montmorency's it would be impossible to
attack him.'[2]

In spite of his recognition that the undertaking
was impossible under existing conditions Condé
still continued to send orders to Montmorency to
attack Nîmes. A letter from Montmorency shows
his exasperation: "If in giving me your commands
it had pleased you to consider the time when I
should receive them and the means which I have

[1] Du Cros, 163; Desormeaux, 303.
[2] Printed by Aumale, III, 515.

to execute them I would very willingly undertake to discharge them. But considering the state in which you ordered me to come into these parts and the time when I received your last letter, I will, if you please, take the liberty to represent to you that it is impossible to carry out your orders, it being more than a week since the harvest has begun and more than six weeks since I informed the King of what was necessary to effect this design, for the execution of which ten thousand men and six hundred horses would not be too many. I have sent your letter to M. de Créquy, who, on my word, will not let me have any of these troops; and besides that they could not have arrived in time, you know, Monseigneur, that I could not have furnished them with supplies, having much difficulty to find subsistence for those whom it has pleased you to destine to serve with me. If it pleases you to give all this your consideration, I dare to hope that you will agree with me and that you will believe, Monseigneur, that everything that can be done in the matter will be done.'[1]

Montmorency kept his word. As soon as reinforcements were forthcoming he set forth with his uncle, the Marquis de Portes, and the Duc de Ventadour to ravage the fertile country near Nîmes upon which Rohan was dependent for his supplies.

[1] Printed by Aumale, III, 520–1.

Had it not been for the vines, olives, and corn from this generous land Rohan and his troops would have been obliged to subsist on chestnuts. Rohan had endeavoured to take advantage of the delay in Montmorency's appearance to start getting the harvest in, but the respite was not long enough, for, though most of the corn had been cut, little of it had been garnered.

Making his headquarters at Marguerites, Montmorency sallied forth to burn the stooks in the surrounding country and to destroy the remainder of the standing crops. Rohan was powerless to prevent the destruction, as Montmorency's forces were now far superior to his. More than fifty hamlets were razed to the ground and the homeless peasants were obliged to take refuge in the neighbouring towns of Nîmes, Uzés, and Alais, where their presence strained the means of supply to the extent of producing a famine. The result of these operations was to cut off the main sources from which Rohan derived both provisions and money.[1]

After a period of indecisive campaigning in which Condé and Montmorency endeavoured, but in vain, to come to grips with Rohan, Montmorency proceeded to lay siege to the Château of Gallargues. Here he had a narrow escape from an inglorious death. As he was going his rounds

[1] *Mercure*, 1628, XIV, 133–9.

K

at midnight a volunteer who was with him accidentally fired off his pistol. The shot missed the Duke, but wounded his horse. Those who were with him were greatly alarmed, especially as the unfortunate gentleman whose clumsiness had caused the accident had a brother who was a supporter of Rohan; but Montmorency himself showed neither anger nor suspicion, and, having caused another horse to be brought, calmly proceeded about his business.[1] On October the 11th Gallargues surrendered unconditionally in spite of the proximity of Rohan's army. Montmorency offered to let all the prisoners go free provided that the neighbouring town and Château of Aymargues were surrendered to him within ten days. But unfortunately Rohan, though fully aware of the terms, refused to surrender the place, and by Condé's orders over sixty Huguenot gentlemen who had been taken at Gallargues were hanged at Montpellier.[2]

This wholesale execution disgusted Montmorency. The wide divergence in their views as to the treatment of prisoners was a constant source of friction between his brother-in-law and himself. Condé wished always to subject them to all the penalties prescribed for rebels and traitors, while Montmorency advocated regarding them simply as prisoners of war. As a result Condé was

[1] Du Cros, 176   [2] *Mercure*, 1628, XV, 61.

PLATE V

HENRY DE BOVRBON *Prince de Conde, Duc d'Anguien et Châuroux, premier Prince du sang, & premier Pair de France Gonuerneur & Lieutenant gñal põ le Roy en ses Pais. et Duches de Berry Bourbonnois Bourgongne & Lorraine &c.*

continually accusing him of compromising the whole
success of the campaign by his tolerance towards
the Huguenots.[1] But in spite of Condé's objections
Montmorency persisted, except in the case of
Chomérac, in granting most generous terms to
the defeated enemy, and, as was his wont, was
scrupulous in observing the terms of the capitulation both in letter and spirit, even when, as after
the fall of Mirabel, he had the greatest difficulty
in restraining his men from reprisals. The only
prisoner hanged on the capture of Mirabel was
a deserter who had betrayed Montmorency's
plans to the enemy and richly deserved his
fate.[2]

Montmorency's generous soul was revolted by
the fate of the prisoners from Gallargues, and he
openly declared that he would willingly have
shed his own blood to save the lives of the victims.[3]
But, as he wrote to Rohan in reply to a letter
asking what action he proposed to take in regard to
the prisoners, he was powerless to save them,
since the matter had been taken out of his hands:
'You may rest assured that I will always cede to
your requests when they do not go beyond my
powers or against my duty, and particularly in
the matter of these poor prisoners from Gallargues
to whom I am naturally favourably disposed,

[1] Aumale, III, 212.   [2] *Mercure*, 1628, XIV, 131.
[4] Aigrefeuille, 393.

since they are of my province . . . but by
command of M. le Prince and in his presence
I have from this morning handed over the
whole management of this matter to M. de
Nesmond, the King's intendant in the armies
of Languedoc. . . .'[1]

In February, 1629, Lunas was taken and Soyon
fell on April the 13th after a siege of ten days.
After a visit to his wife at Beaucaire Montmorency went to Valence in May to meet the King
who had just returned from his campaign in Italy
and on this occasion received him very favourably.[2] It was now decided to proceed against
Privas. Here Montmorency was involved in an
undignified wrangle with Bassompierre. Since
Montmorency was Governor of Languedoc and in
command of the troops, the Maréchal de Schomberg, though his superior in military rank, had
allowed him to take precedence over him at the
Council. But on his arrival Bassompierre refused
to make the same graceful gesture. The King did
not know how to decide between them and,
pending the settlement of the dispute, was reduced
to the expedient of not holding a Council at all.
As soon as the Cardinal arrived Bassompierre
hastened to him and persuaded him to decide
the point in his favour. Montmorency was at
first angry, but he could never bear resentment

---

[1] Printed by Aumale, III, 522–3.   [2] Du Cros, 188.

for very long and a few days later invited Bassompierre to dinner in token of reconciliation.[1]

A very curious incident occurred during the
siege of Privas. Once during a discussion of the
life after death Montmorency and his uncle, the
Marquis de Portes,[2] had solemnly sworn that
whichever of them died first would come to bid
farewell to the other at the hour of his death.
One night when Montmorency was lying asleep
in his tent at Privas he was awoken by the voice
of De Portes sorrowfully bidding him farewell.
Thinking that this was a hallucination due to his
weariness the Duke turned over and went to
sleep again. But he was awoken again by the
same voice, and, growing alarmed, he sent a
messenger to De Portes to enquire after him.
The man he had sent was met on his way by a
messenger from the King bearing the news that
the Marquis had just been shot dead.[3] The loss
of his mother's brother was a great grief to Montmorency, for he had been almost a parent to him
after his own father's death and had looked after
his affairs in the days when the responsibility
would have been too much for him.[4] De Portes
was a distinguished soldier, and on the very day
of his death it had been decided to create him a
Marshal of France.

[1] Bassompierre, IV, 39–45.
[2] Antoine Hercule de Budos, Marquis de Portes.
[3] Du Cros, 191.   [4] Tallemant des Réaux

The Cardinal was at Privas making himself exceedingly unpopular by his persistent efforts to teach the professional soldiers their own business. With characteristic lack of generosity he did his utmost to minimize Montmorency's exploits during his recent campaign. Montmorency seems to have had an unhappy knack of always incurring jealousy wherever he went. Condé too showed a lamentable lack of gratitude for Montmorency's loyal aid.[1] He denounced both Montmorency and Épernon to Richelieu, and this can only have been through jealousy, since they had done all the work and he had shown nothing save incapacity during his tenure of the command. It was in fact mainly through the efforts of Épernon in the west and Montmorency in the east that the rising of the Huguenots had been suppressed.

After the fall of Privas the royal army proceeded to lay siege to Alais. Montauban was the only other place that still held out, and it was whispered that it did so only by arrangement with the Cardinal, who wished himself to take the credit for reducing it. At the siege of Alais Montmorency behaved with his usual reckless gallantry. He himself led an attack on one of the enemy's outposts in the mountains near the town and was injured in the arm by a flying stone.[2] The King, considering that one of the chief officers

[1] Monlaur, 144; Aumale, III, 219.   [2] Du Cros, 194.

in his army had no business to take part in minor
skirmishes just for the pure joy of fighting, sent
to tell him that he was more satisfied with his
courage than with his conduct and that he would
prefer him to carry himself like the general of an
army rather than a simple soldier.[1]

The fall of Alais, which capitulated on June
the 17th, 1629, was so severe a blow to the
Huguenot party that Rohan came to the conclusion that it would be wiser to sue for peace
immediately. Montmorency was not at first permitted to take any part in the negotiations, until
the Huguenots themselves requested that he might
be one of the intermediaries, since they felt that
they could trust him implicitly. And thus it
came about that he played great part in negotiating the Peace of Alais.[2]

After the conclusion of peace Louis XIII
returned to Paris, but the Cardinal still remained
in the south. In the pursuit of his cherished aim
to centralize the government of France under an
all-powerful monarchy Richelieu had for long
been casting jealous eyes on the virtual autonomy
of Languedoc, which, although it had been united
to the French Crown for the last four centuries,
had preserved intact all its local privileges and
franchises. The province possessed its own

[1] *Mercure*, 1628, XV, 494.
[2] Du Cros, 195; Desormeaux, 307-8.

assembly of three Estates which met once a year and voted supplies. Such independence was not in consonance with the Cardinal's schemes and he purposed to undermine it by the issue of an 'Édit des Élus', the ostensible purport of which was that officers were to be elected in the twenty-two dioceses of the province to equalize the distribution of taxation. Actually, however, its effect was practically to do away with the functions of the Estates. While he was at Montpellier he gave orders to enforce the edict. The Estates assembled at Pézénas would have protested, but Montmorency, considering that resistance would be impracticable, for the sake of peace persuaded them to accept it, even though it lessened considerably the power of the Governor of the province and was therefore directly opposed to his own interests.[1]

Richelieu now made a progress through Languedoc. With an enormous suite and accompanied by the Duc d'Elbeuf and the Marshals de Bassompierre, Marillac, and Schomberg he paid a visit to the Duc and Duchesse de Montmorency, who entertained him with great magnificence at La Grange des Prés.[2] Marie Félice had as usual been ill with a hectic fever caused by anxiety for her husband during the recent campaign.[3] She had

[1] Du Cros, 195.
[2] Bassompierre, IV, 57; Rénée, 282; Pitaval, 132.
[3] Du Cros, 186.

remained for the most part at Beaucaire, where
Montmorency had visited her as often as possible,
but he had moved her to La Grange as soon as
it was safe. As always when he was with her the
state of her health speedily improved. The festivities at La Grange, the enormous expenses of which
were entirely borne by the Duke, lasted for nearly
two months. When at last Richelieu decided to
trespass no longer on this truly regal hospitality,
Montmorency accompanied him as far as Montauban to witness his carefully staged triumphal entry
into the town. He did not return to his wife
until he had seen the Cardinal safely out of the
confines of Languedoc.

CHAPTER VII

Montmorency tries to persuade the King to revoke the
edict—The Montmorencys at Chantilly—The King
suspects Montmorency of being in love with the Queen—
Marie de Medici reassures him on this point—Louis XIII
allows Montmorency to retain his blue liveries—The
war in Italy—Montmorency goes as a simple volunteer—
His illness—He joins the Cardinal—His visit to Turin—
He is suspected of frustrating Richelieu's plan to kidnap
the Duke of Savoy—Montmorency appointed to command the army at Pignerol—Delight of the troops—
Precarious condition of the army—The plague—Lack of
supplies—Montmorency asks to be relieved of his command—Louis XIII refuses—D'Effiat appointed to share
the command—The Battle of Veillane—Montmorency's
prodigious exploits—Prince Doria—Montmorency de-
clines to write the official reports of the battle—
D'Effiat concocts reports lauding himself—The King
writes to his mother in praise of Montmorency—
Occupation of Saluces—D'Effiat denounces Montmorency
to Richelieu—Soudeilles gives the Cardinal an account
of the army—Battle of Carignan—Montmorency recalled
—The King's illness—The Cardinal deserted—Montmorency promises to stand by him—Recovery of the
King—Montmorency proceeds to Paris on the affairs
of Languedoc—The Cardinal's affected friendship for
him—He is created a marshal—A banquet at the Hotel
de Montmorency—Quarrel between Montmorency and
Chevreuse—Both the offenders banished to their country-
houses—Montmorency resolves to retire altogether
from the Court—Description of Chantilly.

The province of Languedoc did not submit tamely
to the encroachments of Cardinal Richelieu, and

when the Parlement of Toulouse refused to register
the *Édit des Élus'* the Estates, which had bitterly
resented this tampering with their immemorial
rights, resolved to try to get the whole question
reviewed. Perceiving that the entire province
was united and firm in its opposition to the edict
and that he could count on its whole-hearted
support, Montmorency journeyed to Paris with the
intention of using such influence as he possessed
with the King in persuading him to have the
edict withdrawn.

After a short stay in Paris he retired with his
wife to Chantilly, probably piqued because his
pleas on behalf of the province had been dis-
regarded, though according to some accounts he
was actually ordered to withdraw from Court
by the King, who had been persuaded that his
attentions to the Queen, Anne of Austria, were
too marked. The rumour to this effect is said
to have been started by Richelieu.[1] Whatever
may have been the reasons, it is certain that he
was not at this time on good terms with the King
and that he remained away from Court until the
Queen-Mother, Marie de Medici, persuaded her
son to recall him.[2] Either Louis XIII had never
seriously suspected that Montmorency had been
showing undue attentions to his wife or else the
Queen-Mother had succeeded in reassuring him,

Pitaval, 133.   [2] Desormeaux, 314.

for he received Montmorency quite favourably
on his return, and even went out of his way to
show that he held him in honour.

It was about this time that Louis XIII had
issued an edict forbidding any noblemen to clothe
their households in blue liveries, this being the
royal colour. Although the Montmorency livery
had been blue for years past, the Duke, anxious
not to offend the King, had at once gone to the
great expense of ordering scarlet liveries for the
whole of his immense household. On his return
to Court the King sent for him and told him that
he had not intended the edict to apply to him,
but had been forced to issue it owing to the abuses
and outrages that had recently been perpetrated
in Paris by persons masquerading in blue liveries
similar to those worn by the royal household. He
assured him that it had been far from his thoughts
to deprive him of a privilege which his ancestors
had long enjoyed and told him that he might
countermand the order for the scarlet liveries.[1]

In addition to her civil troubles France was also
at this time involved in a war against the Spaniards
and Austrians in Italy. A French army had
been sent to the help of the Duke of Mantua whose
territory had been invaded by the Austrians.
After peace had been concluded with the
Huguenots Cardinal Richelieu resolved to con-

[1] Pitaval, 133.

duct the Italian campaign with renewed intensity
and raised an army of 40,000 men. Having by
some means persuaded Bassompierre, Créqui, and
Schomberg to consent to serve under him, he
appointed himself generalissimo. Although Montmorency was not given any command he could
not bear to remain inactive at home when there
was any fighting going on and so decided to go
to Italy as a simple volunteer. His example
was immediately followed by the flower of the
southern nobility, who rallied round him at
Lyons.[1] The influx of so many gallant young
men into the city was a source of great joy to
the fair ladies of Lyons, especially as Montmorency
and Bassompierre took it in turns to give balls for
them almost every night.[2]

At the end of January, 1630, the Cardinal left
Lyons to join the army at Grenoble. Montmorency, who for some days had been ill with a
high fever, insisted upon following him the next
day, although he was clearly unfit to travel. The
jolting of the carriage so increased his fever that
he was obliged to call a halt at the Château de
Bressieux, where his host and his attendants
became so alarmed at his condition that they sent
to Grenoble for a doctor to come out immediately.
The messenger, hearing murmurs in the Cardinal's
quarters that the Duke's illness was probably

---

[1] Desormeaux, 317; Cotolendi, 37.   [2] Bassompierre, IV, 77.

'diplomatic', cleverly frustrated this characteristic attempt to blacken Montmorency's character by going to Richelieu himself and requesting him to send his own physician, so that he might bear witness that the Duke's illness was not feigned.[1]

After about a week Montmorency was strong enough to travel again as far as Grenoble, whence a few days later he proceeded to join the Cardinal with the army at Ours (Oulx). Richelieu gave him a flattering welcome and took him with him to Suze (Susa). But as the Cardinal was still occupied with negotiations Montmorency found the inactivity irksome and elected to spend the intervening time at Turin. It is not beyond the bounds of possibility that he had some sort of unofficial instructions to endeavour to influence the Duke of Savoy to throw in his lot with France. An alliance with Savoy was actually Richelieu's chief aim at the moment, but the Duke seemed inclined to wait and see which side won before he decided which side he was on. Montmorency, who always added to the gaiety of any place he went to, was received with a warm welcome by the Duke, who arranged for him to be lodged with great magnificence and honour at the house of the Prince de Carignan. He quickly made himself a great favourite, especially with the feminine part of the Court. The Duke of Savoy averred

[1] Du Cros, 200.

that, since his arrival, the women had become more beautiful and the men more anxious.[1]

It was not long before the Duke of Savoy's indecision began to exasperate Richelieu, and, despairing of ever winning him over in time for him to be of any use, he laid a plan to kidnap him with his family at Revel (Revello) and so force his hand. Somehow or other the Duke was warned in time and evaded the trap. It is alleged that Richelieu suspected, if he did not actually accuse, Montmorency of having given the plot away.[2] If the Duke really did so it must have been because he himself had somehow discovered that such a project was contemplated; he can hardly have betrayed the Cardinal's confidence, for it is impossible to believe that so subtle and experienced an intriguer as Richelieu would have confided a plan of this questionable character to anyone possessing Montmorency's high standard of chivalry and honour.

The fortress of Pignerol (Pinerolo) was captured by cash, Richelieu having judiciously bribed the Governor, but otherwise matters were going very ill for the French. There was a lack of supplies and munitions of war and the army was decimated by disease and famine. Of the troops that remained many were deserting every day. The

---

[1] Du Cros, 201; Desormeaux, 318.
[2] Desormeaux, 320; Rénée, 94.

result, in the words of the chronicler of the *Mercure
François*, was that 'there were few persons of
quality who had any reputation to lose who would
have undertaken the chief command of the King's
army, so fearful were they that their honour would
be shipwrecked by some disaster'.[1]   In this
extremity the King and the Cardinal at a con-
ference at Grenoble then and there resolved to
call in the aid of Montmorency.   On his arrival
the King embraced him warmly, crying: "Here is
the most valiant man in my kingdom!"

Montmorency now accepted the command of
the army at Pignerol (Pinerolo) in succession to
Schomberg.   It was a thankless task that he
was assuming.   His request for supplies and reinforcements was met only with vague promises.
Nevertheless he set forth undaunted.   His arrival
at the end of May, 1630, had the immediate effect
of putting spirit into an army hitherto dismayed
and unsettled by the frequent change of commanders.   The tide of desertions which had begun
to affect even the nobility ceased abruptly.   Well
might Richelieu exclaim with a generosity that was
rare in him: 'There was no discouragement among
the soldiers, since the Duc de Montmorency was
considered courageous, charming, and generous, and
was beloved by the troops.'[2]

[1] *Mercure*, 1630, XVI, 635.
[2] Richelieu, *Mémoires* (Mich et Pouj) VIII, 215.

It was fortunate that Montmorency's wealth enabled him to show his generosity in practice, for no money was available, and he himself was obliged to advance their pay to the troops out of his own pocket.[1] But matters had by now reached such a pitch that even Montmorency, usually so confident, felt himself powerless. The plague was still raging, supplies and reinforcements failed to arrive, and angry criticism of the Cardinal was heard on all sides. Montmorency did all that a man could do. Throughout the campaign in Italy his quarters were open to all comers in need of help, whether officers or common soldiers. He himself showed no fear of the plague, and his own quarters were like a hospital in which the sick were treated by his own doctors.[2] This state of affairs depressed and discouraged him to such an extent that when the King sent for him at St Jean de Maurienne he explained that the condition of the army was beyond all hope and asked to be relieved of his command. Louis XIII refused to release him, but both he and the Cardinal realized that something definite must be done and suggested that he should take command of the army about to cross the Po to relieve Casal (Casale). Before he left, the Cardinal clung to him and cried desperately: "A battle, Monsieur, a battle, in the name of God!"[3]

[1] Du Cros, 205; Desormeaux, 322.
[2] Du Cros, 234; Desormeaux, 341.
[3] Du Cros, 207; Desormeaux, 324.

L

Richelieu's jealousy of Montmorency was so acute that even at this critical time he would not give him a free hand, but did all that he could to hamper him by giving him as a colleague to take command with him on alternate weeks the Maréchal d'Effiat, whom Tallemant des Réaux describes as an ill-educated man who had no knowledge of war. Apart from the essential inexpediency of such an arrangement it was well-known that Montmorency and D'Effiat hated each other, having apparently been rivals in some love-affair in which Montmorency had triumphed.[1] D'Effiat, who was *Surintendant des Finances*, was of a grasping, calculating, envious nature, in vivid contrast to the openness and generosity of Montmorency.

The two commanders set forth at the head of a small army of 7,000 infantry and 800 cavalry.[2] In order to join the main army under the Maréchal de la Force at Javenne (Giaveno) they had to traverse the pass of Veillane (Avigliana), where they knew that the Prince of Piedmont, son of the Duke of Savoy, was waiting for them with far superior forces consisting of 15,000 infantry and 4,000 cavalry. The baggage was got through somehow under cover of darkness and the army itself was to follow on the next morning. The advance

---

[1] Desormeaux, 331

[2] Rénée, 96. Pitaval gives the numbers as 10,000 infantry and 1,200 cavalry. He gives the strength of the enemy's infantry as 16,000.

guard had entered the pass and the rest of the army was about to follow when Montmorency, who was to command the rear-guard and was seated beneath a chestnut tree watching the troops file by, perceived the enemy approaching. 'He gazed on them,' says his chronicler, 'with that noble pride and extraordinary joy which appeared on his countenance whenever some great danger presented itself.'[1]   Some of the officers were in favour of avoiding a battle, but Montmorency was of opinion that they must engage. The reasons for doing so were, he declared, so obvious that he could not waste valuable time in discussing them. He himself was willing to take full responsibility for the decision and ended the council of war abruptly by crying: 'Let him who loves me follow me!' [2]

The original plan was that D'Effiat was to advance with the cavalry while Montmorency supported him with the infantry. But D'Effiat was forced to go by a roundabout way in order to find an easier passage and so had not arrived when Montmorency, who had managed to get his troops across a deep ditch, came face to face with the enemy. Without waiting for help he promptly charged the first squadron of cavalry commanded by Prince Doria, whom he personally wounded and put out of action. Mounted on a huge war-horse, he plunged under heavy fire into the thick of the

[1] Du Cros, 210.   [2] Du Cros, 211; Pitaval, 144.

enemy and had already cut his way as far as their fifth rank before any of his men could follow him, although Soudeilles and several others of his household did their utmost to keep near him.[1] Having thrown this first squadron into disorder, he left the task of completing its defeat to the royal troops behind him, and himself charged the main body of cavalry in the same reckless manner as before. Having struck confusion into them practically unaided, he once more left them to be finished off by those who followed him, and made straight for a German regiment. The Germans, who from afar had witnessed his first wild entry into the battle, were convinced that he must have been killed by now and took him for some sort of an apparition. They were so terror-struck that they turned tail and fled at the very sight of him. It is said that more than three hundred of them fell into a deep ditch filled with water and were drowned.[2] All these prodigious feats Montmorency had performed almost single-handed.[3]

The Duke's great charger, 'La Remberge', had come out of the combat severely wounded and running with gore,[4] but the rider's sole wound

---

[1] Pitaval, 146.

[2] Du Cros, 213; Desormeaux, 329; Cotolendi, 39.

[3] Du Cros was aware that his narrative of Montmorency's exploits at Veillane must seem almost incredible. 'But what I am about to write,' he says, 'is so extraordinary that it will seem as if I am leaving the thread of my history to begin the adventures of a romance.'

[4] Pitaval, 151.

was an insignificant scratch on the lip, though he
had been pretty severely knocked about and must
have looked a sorry sight after the battle. The
pommel of his sword and the straps of his cuirass
had been carried away by musket-shot, his helm
was battered, and the vizor which protected his
face almost cut in half. His arms were so bruised
that they were black for days afterwards.[1]

Among the prisoners was Prince Doria who, on
being brought before Montmorency, at once recognized him as his adversary in the battle and cried:
"*Questo è il signor que m'ha dato le prime ferite.*"
Montmorency treated his illustrious prisoner with
characteristic chivalry. He had him carried to his
own quarters, giving orders that he was to be put
into his own bed and that his surgeons were to
attend him as they would himself.[2] Since Doria
was Montmorency's personal prisoner the Duke
was able to send him to the Château of Beaucaire
to finish his recovery from his wounds as soon as he
was well enough to travel.[3]

With his usual modesty Montmorency declined to
write the official report of the battle or to allow any
of his personal followers to do so. The privilege was
left to D'Effiat, who took full advantage of it to
write an unrestrained panegyric on himself and his
own exploits, hardly mentioning Montmorency at

[1] Du Cros, 213.   [2] Du Cros, 215.
[3] Du Cros, 219; Cotolendi, 40.

all.[1] But it was impossible for him to hope to conceal Montmorency's valour; the whole army was ringing his praises and its voice was heard at Court even before the despatch arrived. "Never was there a finer action; Montmorency performed marvels," said Richelieu,[2] while the King himself wrote to the Duke with his own hand declaring that he felt himself as much obliged by this action as a king could be towards a subject.[3] This was high praise indeed coming from the reserved Louis XIII, but truly on this occasion he does seem to have been stimulated into actual enthusiasm. He wrote to the Queen-Mother, who was then at Lyons.[4]

Madame, the services which my cousin, the Duc de Montmorency, renders me on all occasions oblige me to inform you of the satisfaction I derive from them. While leading my troops into Piedmont, the enemy attempted to attack him on the way; but he charged them so bravely that he left eight hundred of them on the field, took more than twelve hundred prisoners, put the rest to flight, captured nineteen of their standards, and remained master of the field of battle. He has not been

---

[1] Du Cros, 216; Desormeaux, 333. The account in the *Mercure François* is based on D'Effiat's dispatches and, while full of praise for D'Effiat, is disparaging to Montmorency. The opinions of the King and Cardinal here quoted show where the truth really lies.

[2] Richelieu, *Mémoires* (Mich et Pouj) VIII, 233.

[3] Du Cros, 218.

[4] Du Cros, 217; Desormeaux, 334.

wounded at all, thank God, and I have just sent him a special courier to tell him of the gratitude I feel for his services. I beg you to rejoice over them with my cousin, the Duchesse de Montmorency, his wife, and to believe me your very humble and very obedient son, Louis.

Saint Jean, the 12th of July, 1630.

Marie Félice, who had accompanied the two queens to Lyons in order to be as near as possible to her husband, now begged the King to recall him and allow him to rest on his laurels, but Louis informed her candidly that he could not grant her request as it was only because of Montmorency's presence that many remained with the army at all.[1]

Montmorency and D'Effiat now occupied the whole of the marquisate of Saluces (Saluzzo). On July the 20th they entered the town, and the castle surrendered on the following day. Of the prisoners taken on this occasion only the leaders were kept; the rest were freed by Montmorency and sent by him to the Duke of Savoy to bear witness to him of the courage and courtesy of the French.[2] Montmorency appears to have given some of them money to help them get home, and was thereupon denounced to Richelieu by D'Effiat, who did not scruple to hint at treasonable intent in an action which was

---

[1] Du Cros, 233; Monlaur, 151 and 154–5.   [2] Du Cros, 224.

merely inspired by pity and generosity.[1] The Cardinal considered this clemency most improper— and most unnecessary, seeing that the enemy did not return the like civility.[2]

D'Effiat, who had conceived an implacable enmity for Montmorency, did his utmost to injure his colleague in the eyes of Richelieu, and found little difficulty in doing so, since the Cardinal was only too willing to hear ill of him. 'In his despatches,' says Richelieu, 'D'Effiat complained that the Duc de Montmorency, though by nature brave and fearless, possessed so little judgment and so much unsteadiness that what he passionately desired in the morning he would oppose in the evening. . . . This was why the Duc de Montmorency thwarted several excellent projects which the Marquis d'Effiat had put in hand.'[3]

The truth was that Montmorency was so disturbed by the condition of the army that he was reluctant to embark upon any further undertakings. He now sent Soudeilles to St Jean de Maurienne to give the King a true account of the state of the army. Unfortunately Louis XIII had fallen ill and had departed for Lyons so that Soudeilles had to address himself to the Cardinal. He informed his Eminence that the troops were in a desperate condition owing to the plague and to

[1] Monlaur, 155.
[2] Richelieu, *Mémoires* (Mich et Pouj) VIII, 242.
[3] *Ibid*, VIII, 234.

the want of food and all manner of supplies. Food
was so scarce that it had been necessary to go on
shortened rations, and Montmorency himself had
exhausted all his own money in endeavouring to
better conditions and had even sold his own plate
to raise funds to buy food for his troops. Pignerol
was so full of plague that it was a common saying
that birds would drop dead if they flew over the
place. Montmorency himself was ill and D'Effiat
had become as yellow as a ripe quince. In these
circumstances Montmorency asked to be recalled.
Richelieu refused this request. He sent back a
message that the Duke ought to be ashamed of
himself for making it, since if he retreated now he
would lose with ignominy the reputation he had so
gloriously won.[1]

Montmorency now advanced on Carignan (Cari-
gnano). He found the enemy entrenched in a strong
position on the bank of the river Po under Victor
Amadeus, the new Duke of Savoy—his father had
died recently, it is said from chagrin at the capture
of Saluces.[2] After reconnoitring the position with
Soudeilles and one or two others Montmorency
decided to attack in spite of the contrary advice
of the Council of War.[3] Once more he was justified. The enemy were defeated with heavy losses
at comparatively small cost to the French.

[1] Richelieu, *Mémoires* (Mich et Pouj) VIII, 240-1.
[2] *Mercure*, 1630, XVI, 649.
[3] Pitaval, 156.

Although there were many wounded, only three or four officers and some twenty men were killed.[1] Montmorency showed to Don Martino de Aragon, a distinguished Spaniard whom he had taken prisoner, the same chivalrous treatment as he had shown to Prince Doria after Veillane. Overcome by his courtesy Don Martino paid him the highest compliment in his power. "If you were only a Spaniard," he said, "you would be the greatest man in the world."[2]

After the victory of Carignan a truce was negotiated by the papal agent Mazarin, who in later years was to succeed Richelieu. Montmorency, being as usual left out of the peace negotiations, since at their inception D'Effiat had produced from his pocket a document signed by the Cardinal giving him unlimited powers in this matter,[3] was anxious to return to France, and at last Louis XIII ceded to Marie Félice's entreaties and recalled him. On the 24th of September he arrived at Dizimieux, where he purposed to remain for a while in quarantine as he was unwilling to risk carrying the infection of the plague to his friends. But on the very next day the Cardinal de la Valette came with special orders from the King to conduct him straightway to Lyons.[4]

Montmorency arrived to find the King stricken

[1] Du Cros, 231.   [3] Rénée, 102.
[2] Desormeaux, 339.   [4] Du Cros, 235.

with a dangerous fever of the same nature as that
which had wrought such havoc in the army. He
was not expected to live, and it was now that the
Cardinal was able to measure the full extent of the
unpopularity he had created for himself at Court
and among the nobility. Everyone deserted him,
and he himself feared that if the King were to die
he might be banished or imprisoned, if indeed he
could hope to escape with his life.[1] On this
occasion Montmorency once more showed his
nobility of character when he stood by the man
who had done all that he could to injure him.
Some accounts say that Richelieu himself went to
Montmorency and besought him to give him a
refuge in Languedoc if it should become necessary
for him to fly, others that Montmorency of his own
accord made the offer to the Cardinal. It is most
likely that Richelieu asked the King to approach
Montmorency through his favourite, Saint Simon.[2]
At any rate the King sent for Montmorency and
said to him: "My cousin, I require of you two
things: the first that you will serve the State with
the same zeal as you have always shown: the second
that you will love the Cardinal for love of me."
Without hesitation the Duke gave his promise,
and went straight from the King's bedside to seek
the Cardinal, whom he discovered prostrate on his
bed and overcome with despair. The Duke offered

---

[1] Goulas, I, 89–90.   [2] Desormeaux, 346.

to provide him with a refuge should the occasion arise, and Richelieu accepted with alacrity, suggesting the fortress of Brouage as being the most suitable place. Elaborate arrangements including relays of horses all along the road he would have to take were carefully worked out by Montmorency and the Secretary of State, La Vrillière.[1]

Fortunately for Richelieu the King did not die. The abscess in the stomach which was causing all the trouble broke and soon after he was out of danger. With his recovery the star of Richelieu once more ascended.[2]

The Duc and Duchesse de Montmorency now returned to Languedoc for a while. But the troops returning from Italy had brought the plague with them, and the Duke deeming Pézénas unsafe for his wife took her to Balaruc.[3] They were probably there at the time of the *Journée des Dupes*, when another attempt was made to ruin the Cardinal. At any rate they were not concerned in it.[4]

Montmorency had found the province less concerned about the plague and the famine which accompanied it than about the loss of its privileges.[5]

---

[1] Desormeaux, 347; Pitaval, 165.
[2] Desormeaux, 342.
[3] Du Cros, 236; Rénée, 107.
[4] So says Rénée. Du Cros also implies that Montmorency was in Languedoc at the time. Desormeaux on the other hand says that Montmorency was with the King and was one of the few great nobles who stood by the Cardinal.
[5] Desormeaux, 349.

He determined, therefore, to journey once more to Paris to approach the King in the matter. On the borders of Languedoc he left Marie Félice to make the journey by easy stages while he himself travelled post-haste.[1] His reception at Court was for once positively enthusiastic. Even the Cardinal had not yet forgotten the Duke's generous attitude when he was in danger and made much of him, loading him with kindnesses and publicly calling him his son.[2] Compliments such as these cost very little; but when it came to actions Richelieu still showed himself unwilling to do anything that would increase Montmorency's power or influence. His success in the recent campaign made it obvious that he would have to be given high military command in the future, but it would be invidious and difficult to continue to place him over the Marshals of France while he still remained their inferior in military rank.[3] For this reason the Cardinal found it impossible to hinder the King any longer from creating him a Marshal, even though he feared that this honour in addition to his governorship of Languedoc might render him too powerful. The dignity was conferred on him on December the 19th, 1630, and it was remarked that in the patents issued to Montmorency and Toiras at the same time Montmorency was stated to have 'accepted' the dignity

---

[1] Du Cros, 237.   [2] Monlaur, 160.
[3] Du Cros, 238.

of Marshal, while it was 'accorded to' Toiras.
On presenting the Duke with the bâton of his
office the King gracefully said to him: "Accept
it, cousin, you honour it more than it honours
you."[1]

During their stay in Paris the Duc and Duchesse
de Montmorency were forward as usual in offering
entertainment to the Court. Balls or comedies
took place at the Hôtel de Montmorency almost
every day. The Cardinal himself was one of the
sponsors at the christening of Montmorency's
nephew, the Prince de Conti, second son of the
Princesse de Condé, and the celebrations at the
Hôtel de Montmorency were attended by the King,
the two Queens, and the entire Court.[2] The
banquet provided on this occasion was so magnificent and lavish that, although those present took
whole boxes of sweetmeats away with them, the
floor was strewn with those which had been upset
in the confusion and abundance.[3]

It was not long, however, before Montmorency
again fell into disfavour. The occasion was a dispute between him and the Duc de Chevreuse, which
unfortunately took place in the courtyard of the
Château de Monceau where the King was then in
residence. Louis XIII was furious that two of his
chief nobles should dare to draw their swords

[1] Rénée, 108; Monlaur, 160.
[2] Du Cros, 238; Monlaur, 161.
[3] *Mercure*, 1630, XVI, 815.

against each other in his own house and ordered them both to retire to their country-seats and not appear at Court again until they were sent for.[1] Through the influence of Richelieu, who greatly admired the Duchesse de Chevreuse, Chevreuse was recalled a few days before Montmorency. This slight roused Montmorency's bitter resentment, even though he admitted that he preferred being away from the Court. He told the Duc d'Angoulême and the Comte d'Alais who came to visit him at Chantilly that he was weary and disappointed with public life and that he felt, moreover, that by withdrawing he might be able to restore to his wife that peace of mind on which, he was assured, her health depended. He appeared, in fact, to contemplate retiring from an active life of war and politics and remaining with his wife at Chantilly.[2]

Both Montmorency and Marie Félice loved Chantilly and were never happier than when they were there. The beautiful old castle, which had been held by the Montmorencys since the 15th century, was built on a rock in the midst of a wide moat. It was surrounded by wonderful gardens filled with pools, streams, fountains, and waterfalls. The vast woods were thronged with deer. The white hinds, Théophile had said, were the gods of the pools transformed by Sylvie—the name under which he addressed the Duchess.

[1] Du Cros, 247.   [2] Desormeaux, 359–360.

The Princess, when she did devest
Their ancient forms, of new possest,
    A snowy whiteness made them bear:
Kindly bestowing on their grief,
The priviledge of this relief.
    They alwayes should her livery wear.

In another passage in this same poem, *Le Jardin de Sylvie*, he portrays the Duchess fishing:

By chance the Bed I did survey
Whereon a sleeping Naiad lay,
    And Sylvia angling in the Brook:
Then I beheld the Fishes strife,
Which first should sacrifice its life,
    To be the Trophey of her hook.

Marie Félice's favourite spot at Chantilly was a little garden called in her honour '*Le Jardin de Sylvie*'. Here was a little pavilion set upon a lawn which stretched down to a pool fed by a fountain hidden in a shady grove. The surface of the pool was broken by two little green islands planted with orange-trees. Théophile's description of this place is, perhaps, the most charming passage in his poem.[1]

---

[1] The English translation, or rather adaptation, which perhaps exceeds the original in grace and beauty of expression is by Thomas Stanley (1625–1678), a kinsman of Richard Lovelace, and one of the most unjustly neglected of the 17th century lyric poets. His *Sylvia's Park* was published in 1651.

A thousand little Cupids here,
  Aside their Bows and Quivers laid,
When Night is by their eyes made cleer,
  Into the glittering Water wade.
Hither the Nereids resort,
To bath their purer Limbs, to sport,
  And with the Loves raise harmless wars,
Diana from her silver Wain
Descending, leaves her drowsie Swain,
  To swim amongst these naked Stars.

Ith' midst is plac'd a little Isle,
  Crown'd by an Arbours shady Crest,
Where Spring eternal seems to smile,
  With flowers by careful Nature drest.
Hither each morn, and night, repair
The feathered Choristers oth' air,
  To give their various passions vent:
The Nightingale above the rest,
Her joys in this soft language drest,
  Doth to fair Sylvias ear present.

It is small wonder that Montmorency had
resolved that, as soon as the affairs of Languedoc
had been brought to a successful conclusion, he
would retire for ever to this Paradise, where he and
Marie Félice would henceforth lead an Arcadian
existence, adding new beauties to the castle and
gardens and employing their leisure in hunting and

M

fishing. The Montmorencys had always been ardent sportsmen and for such as they Chantilly offered incomparable opportunities of indulging in their favourite pastimes. In the various waters carp, trout, and pike were to be found in abundance, while in the recesses of the great forest roamed wild boar, stags, and roe-deer.

Montmorency was now on the eve of what he hoped would be his last journey to Languedoc. He gaily promised Marie Félice that afterwards the voyage between Paris and Chantilly would be the longest he would ever undertake.[1]

[1] Du Cros, 248; Monlaur, 162.

CHAPTER VIII

The deputies of Languedoc in Paris—Montmorency
acts as intermediary between them and the King—
The Cardinal pretends to reconcile Montmorency and
D'Effiat—Montmorency goes to Languedoc—The royal
commissioners work against Montmorency—General
impression that Richelieu is resolved on Montmorency's
ruin—Hostility between the Cardinal and the Duc
d'Orléans—Gaston appeals to Montmorency for support
—He sends the Abbé d'Elbène to him—Hesitation of
Montmorency—The Cardinal plots to have Montmorency
arrested—Montmorency consents to receive Gaston—
Marie Félice accused of being responsible for her husband's rebellion—Two versions of her actions at this
time—Gaston's premature invasion of France—Montmorency remonstrates with him—Montmorency dis-
closes his true attitude to his wife—His preparations
incomplete—He appeals to the Estates—The declaration
of July 22nd, 1632—Protest of the Archbishop of
Narbonne—Montmorency's desperate efforts to come
to terms—Languedoc unexpectedly remains loyal to
the King—Montmorency's funds seized in Paris—
Arrival of Gaston in Languedoc—Montmorency
meets him at Mauguio—Marie Félice disillusions
Gaston—Failure of the rebels to take Beaucaire—
Montmorency's dispondency—His recollection of a
prophecy.

Since the new financial system instituted by
Richelieu and D'Effiat had signally failed both in
Burgundy and Provence and had been abolished in
those provinces, the people of Languedoc, who had

never become reconciled to the *Édit des Élus*, determined to revive and redouble their protests. When the Estates sent deputies to Paris to represent their views to the King, Montmorency procured them an interview with Louis and himself acted as intermediary in the ensuing negotiations. It was chiefly through his instrumentality that a compromise was arrived at whereby the *élus* were to be recalled and replaced by royal commissioners. Meanwhile the Cardinal was affecting a conciliatory attitude and expressed himself eager to render Montmorency all assistance in his power. He even staged a scene of reconciliation between Montmorency and his implacable enemy D'Effiat, who as *Surintendant des Finances* had been responsible for the unpopular edict. The Cardinal invited them both to a magnificent dinner at Bois-le-Vicomte, where at his instigation D'Effiat plied the innocent and open-hearted Montmorency with insincere protestations of friendship and goodwill.[1]

When the Estates were summoned to ratify the convention agreed upon by their deputies in Paris it was necessary that Montmorency should go to Languedoc to preside over the assembly. It had not been his intention to take his wife with him on this occasion, since he did not intend to remain away for very long; but for some reason or other she displayed an extraordinary reluctance

[1] Du Cros, 245; Desormeaux, 355; Monlaur, 164–5.

to being left behind and was so insistent in her
entreaties that in the end he was forced to give in
and allow her to accompany him.[1]

Montmorency arrived in Languedoc at the end
of October, 1631. He found the whole province
in so dangerous a state of restlessness and discontent
that he deemed it advisable to proceed at once on
one of those progresses of pacification and reassur-
ance which he could carry off so well. As usual
all resentment seemed to fade away everywhere as
soon as he appeared.

On December the 12th the Estates opened under
the presidency of the Duc de Montmorency. The
royal commissioners D'Héméry, Miron, and Verderonne were present. The Estates declared themselves fully satisfied with the convention and afterwards proceeded in state to thank the Duc and
Duchesse de Montmorency for the part they had
played in obtaining it. Outwardly it appeared as
though the whole vexed question had been finally
settled to the satisfaction of all parties, for it did
not at once transpire that there was no intention
on the part of Louis XIII, Richelieu, and D'Effiat
to abide sincerely by the spirit of the agreement.
Miron and Verderonne, at any rate at first, seem
to have been genuinely striving for a reasonable
and pacific settlement, but D'Effiat had all along
determined to make this new system of royal

[1] Baillon, 149; Monlaur, 165-6.

commissioners even more vexatious than the scheme
to which the province had originally objected and
gave instructions to D'Héméry, who was a creature
of his, to raise difficulties at every turn. His
obstructive policy made the Estates more and more
dissatisfied, while Montmorency's resentment increased as it gradually became clear to him that he
had been tricked.[1]

There was a general impression in Languedoc
that Cardinal Richelieu and D'Effiat had set on
foot a subtle campaign to compass the ruin of the
Duc de Montmorency. The King's commissioners
were suspected of being little more than glorified
spies sent for the express purpose of trying to discover defects in his administration of the province.
It was not long before Montmorency himself
discovered that there was some foundation for this
belief. In order to confirm his suspicions he
caused one of D'Héméry's couriers to be stopped
and intercepted his despatches to the Cardinal. By
these he discovered that D'Héméry was denouncing
him to Richelieu. He forwarded the documents
to the Cardinal, with the simple comment that he
considered himself most unfortunate to be treated
in this manner.[2]

Such was the state of affairs when, in the spring
of 1632, the unremitting enmity between the

[1] Du Cros, 251; Desormeaux, 365.
[2] Richelieu, *Mémoires* (Mich et Pouj) VIII, 400; Monlaur, 168.

Cardinal and the King's brother, the Duc d'Orléans, came to a fresh head. There had been open hostility between them ever since the fiasco of the *Journée des Dupes* in the autumn of 1630, when the King had ranged himself more firmly than ever on the side of the Cardinal. After withdrawing for a while to Orléans Gaston had eventually left the kingdom and sought a refuge at Nancy, where, in conjunction with the Duke of Lorraine, he set about making plans for the overthrow of the Cardinal. But Richelieu was too quick for them. In the winter of 1631-2 he struck. A French army under the Marshals de la Force and Schomberg overran the country and forced the Duke of Lorraine to conclude the Treaty of Vic (January, 1632) by which he renounced all foreign alliances directed against France and promised no longer to extend his hospitality to Gaston. But he accepted these conditions under compulsion and never had any intention of keeping his promises. Almost at the same time as the treaty was signed he reaffirmed his alliance with Gaston by secretly giving him his sister, Marguerite of Lorraine, in marriage.[1] Postponing his plans to a more favourable moment, Gaston retired to Brussels to meet his mother, who had made her escape from France and taken refuge there in July, 1631. This was exactly what

---

[1] Gaston's first wife had died in June, 1627, shortly after giving birth to a daughter, Mademoiselle de Montpensier.

Richelieu had wanted; nothing could suit him better than that his two most formidable enemies should thus put themselves in the wrong by open defiance.

In March, 1632, Gaston returned to Lorraine with troops he had succeeded in raising in Brussels. He now issued a manifesto against Richelieu, declaring his intention to enter France at the head of an army and expel him. Casting about him for assistance he bethought him of appealing to Montmorency for support. The time could not have been better chosen; Montmorency had many reasons both public and personal to feel aggrieved against the Cardinal. Not only did he resent Richelieu's attack on the traditional liberties of Languedoc, but he also had every reason for feeling that the Cardinal was an enemy intent upon his ruin. It seemed to him that his forced resignation of the office of Grand Admiral, the execution of his kinsman Bouteville, the recent trial and condemnation of the Maréchal de Marillac in circumstances that could not fail to be alarming to anyone in his own position, could only be regarded as preliminary steps to his own contemplated downfall. Gaston's emissary was thus provided with excellent and abundant material for playing on Montmorency's discontent.

The envoy was the Abbé d'Elbène, nephew of the cunning Alphonse d'Elbène, Bishop of Albi, one of Gaston's most determined partizans. It was, however, only after long hesitation that Montmorency consented to grant him a secret interview at La Grange. D'Elbène possessed a cajoling tongue and much of his uncle's sinister cunning. By the Bishop of Albi's instructions he insisted that Gaston's efforts were directed, not against the King his brother, but solely against his evil advisers and above all against the Cardinal. He made use of the subtle argument that there would be grave danger for France if the heir of a monarch weak in health were forced through lack of support in his own country to throw himself into the hands of Spain, the ancient and hereditary enemy of France. Montmorency's part would be simply to make peace in the royal family, a consummation that could not be attained without the overthrow of the Cardinal. D'Elbène naturally did not fail to lay stress on the fact that all the Cardinal's recent actions obviously showed that he contemplated Montmorency's ruin, and insinuated that the financial measures recently taken in Languedoc were in effect simply part of a design to undermine his influence.[1]

Smarting though he was from his injuries, Montmorency for long held out against the Abbé's specious reasonings; but presently he began to weaken and to examine seriously the possibility of receiving Gaston in Languedoc and then, with

[1] Du Cros, 257;   Pitaval, 176.

the backing of his army, forcing a reconciliation with the King, and consolidating the whole position by a marriage between Gaston and his own niece, the daughter of the Prince de Condé—he was, of course, at this time ignorant of Gaston's clandestine marriage to Marguerite of Lorraine.[1] But he still had scruples as to the political morality of such a course and so caused Gaston to be told that, though in sympathy with his objects, he was reluctant to do any act that could be construed as a rebellion against the King and therefore besought him to seek help elsewhere.

Montmorency's hand was to a certain extent forced by the Cardinal. So convinced was Richelieu that the Duke would end by supporting Gaston that he even attempted to strike prematurely by having him arrested. He authorized D'Héméry and the Marquis de Fossés, Governor of Montpellier, to effect the arrest. In view of Montmorency's popularity in his government Fossés at first thought that the project would be impracticable; but later he came to the conclusion that it might be carried out at a dramatic representation to be given in the Duke's honour by the pupils of the Jesuit College at Montpellier. It was arranged that soldiers were to mingle with the audience and at a given signal to seize the Duke and carry him off to the Citadel, where the garrison would be in readiness to prevent

[1] Goulas, I, 154.

any attempt at rescue. Rumours of the attempt
soon began to leak out and eventually came to the
ears of Montmorency, who at first refused to believe
that any such project could be in contemplation.
But he was speedily forced to believe, for the
matter became common knowledge in the town,
and certain of his supporters came to him and
offered to strike a counterblow by arresting
D'Héméry and Fossés and securing the Citadel.
This Montmorency forbade. He persisted in going
to the play as he had arranged; but Fossés had
thought better of his plan and he was not molested.
Two days later Montmorency left for Pézénas to
join his wife.[1]

Montmorency's knowledge that Richelieu had
contemplated his arrest when he was innocent made
him feel that there was no security to be had and
that his ruin was resolved upon, and this belief
undoubtedly contributed to his fateful decision to
throw in his lot with Gaston. His first sound
resolution to remain benevolently neutral weakened
and he told D'Elbène that he would promise to
support Gaston if he should enter France at the
head of an army sufficiently powerful to afford
the attempt a reasonable chance of success.
D'Elbène assured him that he would appear with
a body of at least 2,000 cavalry and would be supported by 15,000 troops under the Duke of Lorraine.

[1] Desormeaux, 378; Pitaval, 174–5; Rénée, 119.

Montmorency replied that, if he would undertake this, he would be prepared to receive him in Languedoc, provided that he were given time to win over the people and the nobility of the province.

At the time Montmorency's decision to support Gaston was by many attributed to the influence of his wife. D'Héméry actually accused her of being the cause of her husband's rebellion, and Richelieu believed, or at least affected to believe, the accusation, although in his own memoirs he implies that Montmorency needed no such instigation but was from the beginning wholeheartedly eager to receive Gaston.[1] The impression of the Duchess's responsibility was increased because after the tragedy she endeavoured to take the blame as much as possible upon herself and always utterly refused to defend herself publicly against any accusations or insinuations. It is not surprising in the circumstances that most historians have continued to fix the responsibility on her. As a matter of fact it now appears that she knew nothing whatever about Montmorency's intentions until it was too late for her to throw her influence into the other scale, though she tried her utmost to do so even at the last moment. Both her own earliest biographer, Cotolendi, and the Duke's biographer, Du Cros, disculpate her of having had any share

[1] Goulas, I, 152; Richelieu, *Mémoires* (Mich et Pouj) VIII, 399.

in making her husband's decision, and her inno-
cence has been amply proved by her later
biographers, Monlaur, Rénée, and Baillon, who
based their opinions on the manuscript memoirs
of the Soeur Agnes Du Cros, who had heard all
details of the story from the Duchess herself, Madame
de la Barge, her lady-in-waiting, and two of Montmorency's most faithful followers, Soudeilles and
Maurens. The two last, at any rate, since they
adored Montmorency, would scarcely have admitted
that he alone was to blame, if it had not been so.
This should dispose of Pitaval's contention that
the Duchess had been whitewashed by her early
biographers. He asserted that they were acting
under the inspiration of the nuns of the Visitation
who regarded her as a saint and desired that all dark
passages in her life should be rigidly suppressed.[1]
However this may be, there certainly exist two
circumstantial but diametrically opposed accounts
of Marie Félice's actions at this time. That which
is unfavourable to her relates that Montmorency
would have refused even to see D'Elbène if it
had not been for his wife's insistence. It also gives
an account of a conversation between the Duke
and the Duchess supposed to have been overheard
by one of her maids who used to sleep at the bottom
of her bed. After a long discussion in which the

---

[1] It should be emphasized that Rénée, Baillon, and Monlaur, writing
in the 19th century, were in possession of additional information
unknown to Pitaval in the preceding century.

Duchess had urged her reluctant husband to join
Gaston he at last gave in saying: "Well, Madame,
you wish it: I will do it to please your ambition,
but remember it will cost me my life." When the
Duchess tried to enter into further protestations
he interrupted: "Let us speak no more of it, Madame,
it is decided. I shall not be the last to repent of it."[1]

Considering that Marie Félice had from her first
coming to France steadfastly kept out of all
political intrigues, considering that, in spite of her
devotion to the Queen-Mother, it had been she who
on a former occasion when Marie de Medici had
appealed to Montmorency for help had persuaded him
to remain loyal in his allegiance to Louis XIII,
considering above all the mental and bodily agonies
she always suffered when her husband was in
any sort of danger, it seems far more probable
that the opposite account is the true one and that
she really was kept in ignorance of his plans by
Montmorency.

The Duke would in any case have had an
additional reason for endeavouring to conceal his
plans from her, since she had been very ill since
her return to Languedoc. As always he looked
after her with the tenderest care, carrying her in
his arms from one bed to another frequently so as
to refresh her and cool her fever.[2]

---

[1] Pitaval 178–9. He is in some measure supported in his view of
Marie Félice's responsibility by Desormeaux (373–4).

[2] Monlaur, 167.

According to the other, and perhaps even more circumstantial account the Duc de Montmorency, in the hope of concealing everything from his wife, remained at her bedside all day and held all his consultations at night, which he could manage the more easily because he was occupying a separate bedchamber during his wife's illness.[1] But it was impossible to continue for ever to hide from Marie Félice that something was toward. She heard rumours that Gaston had entered the kingdom at the head of an army and began to connect them with the coming and going of mysterious messengers and the atmosphere of intrigue in which her husband had recently become enveloped. When her anxious heart had divined all, her agitation was extreme. On three separate occasions, weak as she was, she made her women dress her and take her to her husband, when she threw herself on her knees before him and besought him tearfully not to engage in an enterprise which was bound to bring death in its train. The Duke assured her gently that he would do nothing without long consideration before-hand and that at any rate he had no intention of engaging in a rebellion.[2]

When Montmorency had promised his help to Gaston it had been on the understanding that he would make considerable preparations and assure himself of substantial assistance before

[1] Cotolendi, 47.   [2] Monlaur, 175.

embarking on so hazardous an enterprise. He never imagined that he would descend upon him, as he did, suddenly and prematurely with the exiguous remnants of a defeated army which at the best of times had not been large. Gaston had not been fortunate. On entering Lorraine at the head of several regiments he had at once been joined by the Duke of Lorraine; but in the very first engagement with the French army the Duke of Lorraine's troops had been soundly trounced, and the Duke himself had thereupon very wisely decided to retire from the conflict and had made peace by the Treaty of Liverdun. Gaston should have done the same. Instead, although deprived of the support of Lorraine and not receiving the help he had hoped for from the Emperor and the King of Spain, both of whom had their hands full elsewhere, he was rash enough to enter Burgundy in June at the head of some two thousand horse mostly consisting of German and Walloon mercenaries and adventurers.[1] With Schomberg and La Force close at his heels he marched across France in the forlorn hope of picking up support by the way. The town of Dijon refused to receive him within its gates and every other town he approached followed suit.[2] In despair he pressed on to Languedoc, sending an urgent message to Montmorency: "I am appealing to you

[1] *Mercure*, 1632, XVIII, 506; *Life of Épernon*, 492.
[2] *Mercure*, 1632, XVIII, 506–513.

PLATE VI

GASTON *fils de France, Duc d'Orleans, de Chartres, de Valois, et d'Alençon, Comte de Blois, de Montlehery, et de Limours, Gouuerneur de Languedoc, Lieutenant Gn͞al. du Roy son nepueu par toute la France, Chef de ses Conseils, et General͞me de ses armées, nasquit a Fontainebelleau le 25. Apuril 1608. de Henry le Grand, et de Marie de Medicis son espouse.*

A Paris chez B. Moncornet Auec priuilege du Roy

as to my last refuge : you can save me without losing yourself : I am coming to throw myself in your arms."[1]

On receipt of this message Montmorency sent Soudeilles to Gaston informing him that he was not ready and could not possibly receive him till the end of August.[2] Soudeilles no doubt discharged the task with a good will, since he was one of the few about Montmorency who had done his utmost to prevent him from joining Gaston. At the time when the Court had been uncertain which way Montmorency would declare himself Richelieu had sent Soudeilles, who happened to be at Court, to Montmorency to endeavour to persuade him to remain loyal. It is said that Soudeilles was at first successful in shaking Montmorency's determination, but that in the end his wise counsels were overcome by the superior eloquence and subtle persuasions of the Bishop of Albi and his nephew. Montmorency had sadly said to Soudeilles : "My friend, the die is cast ; there is no longer time to draw back. I have given my word."[3] And now Soudeilles' last hope had gone, for Gaston informed him that he could wait no longer and sent him back to Montmorency to announce his approach.

Montmorency realized that the time had come when he could not possibly hide the matter any

---

[1] Baillon, 156.   [2] Goulas, I, 176–8.
[3] Desormeaux, 379–380.

longer from his wife. He came gravely into her bedchamber and requested her to dismiss her women that he might be alone with her. Somehow she knew instinctively what it was that he had to say to her, and she was so overcome that she could not wait to hear, but fell back on the pillows in a dead faint. Montmorency hastily summoned assistance and remained with her till she came out of her swoon, when he retired without having dared to reveal what he had come to tell her. As he came slowly from her apartment he looked so downcast that several of his gentlemen asked in alarm whether he had changed his mind about supporting Gaston. The Duke shook his head and replied that it was now too late. But he had been unnerved by his wife's obvious terror and distress and he shut himself up in his room and refused to see anyone.[1]

The next morning, when Marie Félice was better and calmer, Montmorency went to her again and showed her the letter he had received from Gaston. Gently he told her his reasons for acting as he had done and enlarged upon the prospects of success. But Marie Félice was not to be reassured or comforted. With tears streaming from her eyes she cried: "Alas! if I was so afraid when I saw you serving the King, how afraid shall I be when I see you in arms against him." Although Mont-

[1] Monlaur, 176.

morency did his best to comfort her, assuring her
that his real intentions were very different from
what they appeared on the surface and from what
would be publicly thought of them, he himself
could not avoid being affected by her grief and as
soon as he could cut short the painful interview.[1]

Gaston's imminent arrival in spite of repeated
remonstrances and some two months before the
time arranged set all Montmorency's plans awry.
His preparations were scarcely even begun. Not
one of the twenty-four regiments upon which he
had counted was under arms, and a sum of five
hundred thousand livres which he had caused to
be raised for him in Paris in order to finance the
rising had not yet arrived. None of the promises
Gaston had made to Montmorency had been kept,
and many of his friends and advisers were of the
opinion that he was no longer bound by his promise
to Gaston and would have been perfectly justified
in withdrawing it.[2] But Montmorency decided not
to repudiate his promise of support, since, if he did
so, Gaston would inevitably be forced to place himself in Spanish hands and to seek help from France's
bitterest enemy, whose motives would be very
different from those of Frenchmen who, like himself, were simply discontented with the existing
government.[3] It seemed to him that the best

[1] Monlaur, 176–7; Baillon, 158; Rénée, 120.
[2] Goulas, I, 176.   [3] Rénée, 125.

course open to him was to appeal to the Estates.
On July the 22nd, 1632, he laid before them the
declaration that was to be his ruin. The Estates
did not disappoint him. By an almost unanimous
vote they agreed to receive Monsieur in Languedoc
and authorized Montmorency to raise troops and
contributions. The nobles and the ecclesiastics
came in partly through loyalty to Montmorency
himself and partly through local patriotism and
hatred of Cardinal Richelieu. The favourable vote
of the third estate was secured by the persuasions
and bribery of the Bishop of Albi.[1] Almost the
only voice raised in protest was that of the Archbishop of Narbonne. Immediately after the declaration Montmorency caused the Archbishop and the
King's commissioners to be arrested; but this was
simply a precautionary measure and they were not
detained for long.[2]

Although the Archbishop of Narbonne had done
his utmost to prevent the rising he was far from
being Montmorency's enemy; on the contrary he
showed himself well-disposed towards him and
anxious to do all in his power to save him from the
consequences of his folly.[3] As soon as he had been
released he hastened to Lyons to try to persuade
the King to work for a pacific solution. Louis

[1] Pitaval, 181.
[2] Goulas, I, 179; Desormeaux, 382; Richelieu, *Mémoires* (Mich et
Pouj) VIII, 401.
[3] Desormeaux, 376; Rénée, 119.

XIII seemed to lend a favourable ear to his arguments and authorized him to open negotiations
with Montmorency.[1] Whether it was by the Archbishop's advice or no it is certain that Montmorency
did make desperate efforts to obtain peace without
bloodshed. He wrote to his nephew, the Comte
d'Alais, who was with the Court, informing him of
his grievances against Cardinal Richelieu, but
affirming his loyalty to the King and declaring that
he was even now ready to lay down his arms and
force Gaston to make peace provided only that he
were allowed to go free.[2] If it were considered
expedient he would be willing to quit the kingdom
and take service for a while in the German wars
under Gustavus Adolphus of Sweden.

All his advances were rejected. The Cardinal was
determined that he should not be allowed to escape.
He affected to believe that all Montmorency's pro-
fessions were insincere and that he was simply trying
to gain time to strengthen his party and complete
his preparations before the King could arrive [3]
Since he had no misgivings as to the ultimate result
of the rising Richelieu flatly refused to make con-
cessions of any sort. He was resolved not to make
a premature peace which would save the man upon
whose ruin he had determined.

[1] Pitaval, 192.
[2] Desormeaux, 387; Richelieu, VIII, 401.
[3] Richelieu, *Mémoires* (Mich et Pouj) VIII, 408.

Although the Estates had declared for Gaston practically the whole of Languedoc somewhat unexpectedly remained loyal to the King. The sympathies of the province seem to have been with Montmorency and there can be little doubt that if he had had all the time he had asked for Languedoc would have been solidly behind him.[1] But, as it was, the prospect that the rebellion would prove successful was too slender. The two royal armies under Schomberg and La Force were fast approaching in pursuit of Monsieur, and, moreover, owing to the efforts of Épernon, the neighbouring provinces had already declared their loyalty to the King. Of the chief towns of Languedoc only Béziers, Alais, Lunel, and Albi declared for Gaston and Montmorency; all the others, including Nîmes, Narbonne, Montpellier, and Beaucaire, remained loyal to the King.

The failure of Languedoc to rise was not the only disastrous consequence of Gaston's premature arrival. It also had the effect of cutting off financial supplies. At the first news that Montmorency was supporting Gaston the Hôtel de Montmorency in Paris was seized by order of the Cardinal. In it was found the money, 550,000 livres, ready to be despatched to finance the revolt. This was promptly confiscated.[2]   In order to raise the neces-

---

[1] Goulas, I, 180.
[2] *Mercure*, 1632, XVIII, 520; Richelieu, *Mémoires* (Mich et Pouj) VIII, 404.]

sary money by some other means Montmorency
was urged to seize all the goods at the fair of Beaucaire, which was then being held, and to force the
owners to repurchase them.   He flatly refused, even
on the plea of urgent necessity, to commit an action
which he deemed both mean and dishonourable.[1]

When the Cardinal was informed of his squeam-
ishness he was hugely delighted.   "This shows that
God has struck him with blindness," he said, "and
that the Magdalene, the protectress of the kingdom,
has rendered fruitless a rebellion started on the day
of her feast."[2]

In the meantime Gaston had arrived.   Lodève,
a small town on the borders of Languedoc, was the
first place in France to open its gates to him.   From
here he sent the Comte de Brion to announce his
arrival to Montmorency who was then at Gignac.
Montmorency did not mince his words; he informed
the messenger straight out that Monsieur had
ruined everything by his ill-timed appearance and
that his cause was as good as lost already.

Shortly after, Montmorency met Gaston at
Mauguio.   Montmorency was of the opinion that
their best course would be to attempt to gain
possession of Nîmes, but the plan was frustrated
by La Force, who was able to throw troops into
the town before they could arrive.   Montmorency
then decided to proceed to Beaucaire to endeavour

---

[1] Du Cros, 260; Desormeaux, 384.   [2] Richelieu, VIII, 404.

to secure the Château ; since he had reason to believe that the Governor was still hesitating whether to declare for him or not. Meanwhile Gaston went to Béziers, where one of his first acts was to wait upon Marie Félice to render her his grateful thanks, the Bishop of Albi having informed him that it was entirely through her influence that Montmorency's support had been secured. To his unbounded astonishment he found that he had been deceived in this particular. The Duchess left him under no illusion as to her true feelings. "Monseigneur," she said to him when he attempted to thank her, "if the Duke my husband had been able to defer to the counsels of a woman, I cannot conceal from you that assuredly Your Royal Highness would not be here."[1] Gaston himself afterwards confessed that he was struck to the heart by her attitude and that he could only promise that he would endeavour to make amends by doing all in his power to care for her husband's life.

After some delay Montmorency had won over the Governor of the Château of Beaucaire, but was chagrined to find that the town still remained unfavourable to him. Deeming it necessary to secure the place, he sent for Gaston's troops. Considering the smallness of the place and the weakness of the garrison it would have been a comparatively simple matter to gain possession of it if a bold stroke had

[1] Baillon, 159; Monlaur, 177.

been attempted. But a dispute arose between Montmorency and the Duc d'Elbeuf as to who should take command, and Gaston had not enough courage or decision to settle the matter one way or the other. While valuable time was wasted in useless argument a regiment from Tarascon across the Rhone managed to enter the town and relieve the besieged.[1]

During the month of August the rebels remained at Béziers, where in spite of the shadow hanging over them the time was spent in gaiety. While those around him flirted, danced, and attended banquets and concerts Montmorency alone remained aloof and took no part in any of the festivities. He could not even be persuaded to dance, he who was accounted the best dancer in all France. A gloom had settled over him, and he seems to have realized even now that there was no hope left for him.[2] To the Comte de Gramont he wrote shortly after Monsieur's arrival: 'All that I can tell you is that I am with Monsieur, the King's brother, my ill fortune having reduced me to not being secure of life or even of liberty. The Estates have joined us so we are not ill accompanied.'[3]

The two armies which had dogged Gaston's footsteps ever since he entered France were now fast approaching. That under La Force had followed

---

[1] Richelieu, VIII, 402; *Mercure*, 1632, XVIII, 741–751.
[2] Goulas, I, 182–3.   [3] Rénée, 121.

him down the Rhone, while the other under Schomberg had cut across to Toulouse, the object being eventually to catch the rebels between two fires. Moreover, as soon as the news of Montmorency's defection had come to Court the King and the Cardinal had set forth for Languedoc. By a proclamation dated August the 23rd Montmorency and the whole of Monsieur's party were formally declared guilty of high treason.[1] Well might Montmorency ponder over a prophecy made by an astrologer, who cast his horoscope at the time of his birth and foretold that he would equal or surpass his illustrious ancestors in glory if he could survive his thirty-eighth year, when a great calamity would threaten him.[2]

[1] *Mercure*, 1632, XVIII, 530–5 and 545–552.
[2] Goulas, I, 177. Goulas had the story from one of the Bishop of Albi's family.

CHAPTER IX

The rebels resolve to attack Schomberg—Montmorency
takes leave of his wife—Schomberg advances on
Castelnaudary—Montmorency doubts Gaston's courage
—The Comte de Moret—The Comte de Rieux—Battle
of Castelnaudary—Moret charges the enemy—Montmorency follows suit—His horse falls on him—With-
drawal of the Orléanist troops—The royal troops reluctant
to take Montmorency prisoner—Montmorency summons
St. Marie to his aid—St. Preuil and Pontis extricate
the wounded Duke—He is disarmed by the soldiers
—The story of the bracelet—Schomberg's grief—
Montmorency carried to Castelnaudary—Emotion of
the inhabitants—Montmorency refuses the aid of
Schomberg's surgeon—Arrival of his own surgeon,
Lucante—Montmorency's wounds—He discusses the
battle with the soldiers—He is visited by Soudeilles—
A friendly message from Epernon—No attempt by
Gaston to rescue Montmorency—Toulouse refuses to
accept the responsibility of guarding Montmorency—
Schomberg's anxiety.

The last hope of the rebels in Languedoc was
to prevent the junction of the two royal armies
and to engage with each separately. Schomberg,
who was advancing towards Castelnaudary, was the
nearer, and it was decided to attempt to put him
out of action before the arrival of La Force.

On August the 24th Montmorency took leave of
his wife. She was still very ill and weak and he

sat by her bedside for several hours trying to cheer and comfort her. After the battle was over and won, he said, he would be in a position to attain his aim, the reconciliation of the King and his brother. He was convinced that God, aware of his plans, would not refuse his aid. Then, when success had crowned his efforts, he would return to her for good and all. Poor Marie Félice had heard this promise so many times before. She was overwhelmed by her emotion and threw her arms round her husband, clinging to him as if she feared to let him go. "I expect everything of God's mercy," she cried, "but I fear your own courage. Fear it yourself, I implore you. Take good care of your poor heart, as I have not been able to keep my dear soul with me." By this time she was near to fainting. She tried to smile; but her eyes closed and she sank back on her pillows in one of her customary swoons.[1]

Montmorency himself was so moved by this scene that it was with the utmost difficulty that he managed to control himself while he was still with Marie Félice. As soon as he stepped outside her room he too fell to the floor in a dead faint. His squires who hastened immediately to his aid had some difficulty in reviving him. When he came to, he fell on his knees and prayed aloud: "O God, I pray thee that all the misfortune of this enter-

[1] Monlaur, 180–1.

prise, if it must come, may fall on my head, that my wife may be spared the blow, and that my eternal salvation may not perish with my life."[1]

The first move in the campaign had been won by Schomberg, who after a few days' siege had taken the Château of St Félix de Caraman, which had been held for Gaston with a mere handful of men by a gentleman of the country named Du Maillard and his brothers. Schomberg then advanced towards Castelnaudary which had remained loyal to the King. His army consisted only of some six to seven thousand men, while Gaston had superior numbers. With thirteen thousand men he lay some three leagues away from Schomberg's forces. The country between the two armies was marshy and intersected by several streams.[2]

As a precautionary measure against attack Schomberg set up an observation post in an empty house situated among the vineyards. Montmorency took it without difficulty and posted a hundred and fifty men there. This slight setback rendered Schomberg all the more cautious. He was anxious not to engage until he had manœuvred himself between Gaston's army and Castelnaudary. To do this he would have to cross the river Fresquel which at present separated both armies from the town.

As always, Montmorency had immediately recovered his spirits in the face of danger and, greatly

[1] Monlaur, 182; Baillon, 158.   [2] Pontis, 179.

encouraged by the success of his preliminary brush with the enemy, returned gaily to Gaston. "Oh, Sir, the day is now come," he cried, "that will make you master of your enemies, and bring the Son and the Mother together again, but——" he added, pointing to his sword, "we must dye this up to the hilt in blood." Gaston took this remark as an aspersion on his courage and heatedly replied: "Ho, Monsieur Montmorency, you will never leave your blustering. You have promised me mighty conquests a long time, but I still see nothing but hopes. I would have you know, that I for my part can make my peace, and retreat whenever I please, and make a third man."[1]

Montmorency was indeed somewhat doubtful of the courage and still more of the reliability of the King's brother. He went apart with his friends, the Comte de Rieux, the Comte de Moret, and Monsieur de Chaudebonne and confided his doubts to them. "Our young spark is turned coward," he said, "he talks of securing himself and making a third man, but neither you Monsieur de Moret, nor you Monsieur de Rieux, nor I will show him the way, and we must engage him so far now that he shall be forced to fight to-day whether he will or no."[2] The events of the day

[1] Sic in Cotton's translation of Pontis. The original French is *me retirer moi troisième*. The meaning is not clear.

[2] This incident is related by Pontis (179 *et seq*) who says that he had it from Aiguebonne, Chaudebonne's brother.

were to show how much reason Montmorency
had for his doubts of Gaston's courage and for
his confidence in that of young De Moret and
old De Rieux.

Antoine de Bourbon, Comte de Moret, was the
son of King Henri IV by Jacqueline de Breuil.
Legitimated in 1608, the year after his birth, he
had originally been destined for the church, but
had preferred the career of arms. It is curious
that a man of his bold and gallant character should
have chosen to throw in his lot with the pusillanimous Duc d'Orléans, but so he had done. Through
all the vicissitudes of the past few years he had
remained at his side and had loyally accompanied
him on this forlorn expedition from Lorraine. De
Rieux was a man of a different stamp. Although
himself justly renowned for bravery, his was a cool
and considered courage and he strongly deprecated the gay recklessness of Montmorency, whom
he had known since he was a child and loved with
a father's love. He now earnestly besought him
not to expose himself unnecessarily in the forthcoming fight. Montmorency merely smiled sadly,
and perhaps the older man perceived the despair
that was in that smile, for he simply said:
"Monsieur, I will die with you."

The accounts of the Battle of Castelnaudary,
though fairly numerous, are somewhat conflicting,
chiefly owing to the desire of every narrator to

thrust into prominence his own part in the events.[1]
The whole action hinged on the fact that to reach
Castelnaudary it was necessary for Schomberg to
cross the river Fresquel. Montmorency's plan was
to await Schomberg at a certain long narrow
bridge, which was believed to be the only practi-
cable means of crossing the river, and there to prevent the passage of the enemy, or, as Schomberg
himself thought, to let half his army cross and
then fall on the rearguard.[2] Schomberg, however, was able to frustrate this plan. When a
body of his cavalry had discovered that the bridge
was being held the Marshal decided to cross the
river at another point by a little-known ford that
had been pointed out to him by a gentleman of the
locality.[3] He sent Savignac, Captain of the Guards,
to secure this passage, and shortly after he himself crossed with his troops and drew them up in
order of battle on the plain at the foot of the hills
on which the town was situated. There seems to
be little doubt that Montmorency was out-

---

[1] The account of the battle here given is based chiefly on the evidence
of the military witnesses at Montmorency's trial (contained in the
manuscript in my possession) and on the three accounts given in the
Mercure François, 1632, XVIII, 558–580. These consist of Schomberg's
official report and independent accounts written by cavalry captains
in the opposing armies. The other references given here are to be
regarded as supplementary.

[2] Mercure, 1632, XVIII, 558–565 (Schomberg's report).

[3] Most of the accounts imply that there was a second bridge.
Desormeaux (389) says that it was a ford. This version is confirmed
by Richelieu, who adds that the ford was discovered by his brother-
in-law, the Marquis de Brézé, in command of the advance-guard.
(Mémoires, VIII, 409).

manœuvred by him and was not expecting to
see him where or when he appeared. All the
evidence goes to show that he was on a reconnoitring expedition on the further bank of the river
when he fell in with the enemy's outposts. Pontis
asserts that he fell into a carefully prepared am-
bush, but, besides that Schomberg says nothing of
this, the evidence of all the witnesses at the subsequent trial indicates that he merely fell in somewhat prematurely with the advanced guards of
Schomberg's army, and that instead of retreating
and allowing the main body of the Orléanist forces
to come up he recklessly decided to engage. Of
Montmorency's responsibility there can be no
doubt; he behaved more like a heedless volunteer
than an experienced general. The day at Castelnaudary was lost, according to Goulas, solely owing
to Montmorency's imprudence, "a rashness," he
remarks, "ridiculous in a man of his age and rank."[1]

Montmorency had not yet put on his full battle-
armour and was not riding his charger, but was
mounted on a gaily caparisoned little barbary
horse adorned with red, white, and blue plumes.
When he and his small body of cavalry were fired
on by Savignac's musketeers several of his followers were wounded and their ranks were thrown
into confusion. Prudence would have recom-
mended a speedy retirement, but even though it

[1] Goulas, II, 199.

o

had been definitely arranged that no engagement
should take place until the rest of the troops with
the artillery had come up, the impetuous Comte de
Moret at once charged the enemy at the head of
his troop.[1] That anyone in the world should take
the lead over him in going into battle was more
than Montmorency's pride could bear, and he also
gave the order to charge. Moret fell at once, and
his death, instead of checking Montmorency, made
him all the more eager to engage. He called out
to De Rieux: "Come, Monsieur de Rieux, my good
friend, let us attack boldly; fighting has begun on
the left wing."

Followed by no more than five or six gentlemen,
among whom was De Rieux, who fell mortally
wounded almost immediately, Montmorency leapt
a ditch under a hail of bullets and charged the
enemy. The Seigneur de Beauregard, Captain of
a company of light horse in the royal army, relates
that with two companions he attacked Montmorency just after he had come through the infantry fire. Montmorency fired at him, but his
cuirasse deflected the bullet, which hit his left arm
and broke it. He himself then fired two balls at
Montmorency and hit him in the throat. But
Montmorency succeeded in getting past him and
engaged with the Baron de Laurières and his son,

---

[1] Du Cros, 263; Desormeaux, 389. The author of *Mémoires de
feu Mr le Duc D'Orléans* attributes the premature beginning of the
battle entirely to the rashness of Moret.

the Baron de Bourdet. He unhorsed the father
and wounded the son with a vigorous blow which
pierced his helmet.[1]

Though wounded by all three of these antagonists
Montmorency pressed on and charged the infantry.
He battered his way through six ranks and had
reached the seventh when he suddenly realized
that he was alone in the midst of the enemy and
tried to cut his way out to rejoin his own people.[2]
Had he been mounted on his great powerful war-
charger he would no doubt have been successful,
but his gallant little horse had received a generous
share of the blows that had been directed against
the rider, and just as he was getting clear it fell
dead and rolled on top of him. Montmorency was
so weak from loss of blood flowing from his many
wounds that he was unable to get free. According
to some accounts another dead or injured horse
had fallen partly across his own mount thereby
rendering the process of extricating himself still
more difficult for one in his weak condition.

By this time it had become clear to those about
the Duc d'Orléans that Montmorency must either
have fallen or been taken prisoner. The Vicomte
de Poujol was anxious to attack the royal forces
again, but could not get the cavalry to follow him.
Another brave man, the Comte de Brion, actually
attempted to go forth by himself in search of

[1] Du Cros, 263.   [2] Desormeaux, 391.

Montmorency, and was forcibly restrained by his companions.[1] The disappearance of Montmorency so disheartened the Orléanist troops that they withdrew, leaving the field to Schomberg. The pity of it is that any attempt to rescue Montmorency would have been welcomed by the enemy.[2] For at least a quarter of an hour the King's soldiers, officers and men alike, although they knew perfectly well where he lay, affected not to notice him in the hope that some of his own people would come and carry him off. But no one came, and at last for his own sake they were obliged to go to his assistance themselves, especially as he himself was calling on them for aid. Being afraid that in his helpless position he might be pillaged by some of the unscrupulous soldiery he called to one St. Marie, Sergeant in the Royal Guards in the company of St Preuil. He begged St Marie, who had formerly served under him, not to abandon him and to obtain a confessor for him. He also summoned Boutillon, another Sergeant in the Guards known to him. St Marie went to Pontis, an officer in his regiment, and informed him that he had seen Monsieur de Montmorency lying wounded beneath his horse. Pontis, who was friendly towards the Duke, was very reluctant to be the one to take him prisoner and in his turn informed his superior officer, St Preuil. But St Preuil was in

[1] Du Cros, 264–5.   [2] Puységur, I, 128.

the same position and also refused to go alone.
Finally they decided to go together with a few
soldiers including St Marie.[1]

When they came to the spot where the Duke lay
St Preuil knelt beside him with an exclamation of
pity.   Montmorency had formerly had a quarrel
with this officer and feared that he would now
welcome an opportunity of doing him an injury.
So he cried out: "Come not near me, I have life
enough left to kill thee still."   But to do the Duke
any hurt was far from St Preuil's thoughts and he
and Pontis managed to reassure him as to their
intentions.   They had the greatest difficulty in
extricating him from the ditch into which he had
fallen, as his thigh was jammed beneath the dead
horse.   When they drew him out he was covered
from head to foot with blood, which flowed also
from his mouth owing to the severe wound in the
throat he had received at the hands of Beauregard.   St Preuil knelt in tears beside him   and
cried: "Courage, master!"   Since the fighting had
not yet ceased St Preuil and Pontis were not able
to remain with the wounded Duke, and so gave
orders to St Marie to look after him.   At Montmorency's own request St Marie and Boutillon, with
the aid of several other soldiers, disarmed him in
order to give him air.   While they were removing

[1]Pontis, 179.   His account is borne out by that of the Captain in
the royal forces given in the *Mercure François*.

his helmet, his cuirass, and his buff leather collar which had been pierced in several places, Montmorency took a ring off his finger and handed it to St Marie, begging him if he died, as he was sure he would, to cause it to be delivered to the Duchess. The Duke's body-armour was given to Bourguignon, St Preuil's lackey, to look after, while Boutillon took charge of his weapons.

In the meantime several other officers had come up including the Sieur d'Espénan, who whispered to Boutillon to carry the Duke away as quickly as possible. Four soldiers hastily made an improvised litter out of their own cloaks and were preparing to carry the Duke away when the Marquis de Brezé, Cardinal Richelieu's brother-in-law, came up and asked St Marie who the prisoner was. On being told he approached Montmorency and said: "Courage, Monsieur, it is nothing." He then gave orders to hasten the transport of the wounded Duke.

There is a story that while Montmorency was being borne towards Schomberg's tent the gentlemen walking beside the litter perceived on his arm a diamond bracelet containing a portrait of the Queen. Thinking that it might compromise him, they endeavoured to get it away from him. One of them, Monsieur Pomponne de Bellièvre, a magistrate and intendant in the royal army, actually succeeded in detaching it. The Cardinal

was afterwards informed of this incident by one of
his spies who had been present, and is reported to
have made use of it to poison the King's mind
against Montmorency.[1]

The wounded Duke was carried straight to
Schomberg, who was extremely affected at the
sight of him and declared that he would have been
willing to shed his own blood rather than see him
in this misfortune.[2] Montmorency at once asked
for a confessor and was attended by Schomberg's
own almoner. He was also given some refresh-
ment and the wounds in his face and neck were
temporarily dressed by the surgeon of the King's
company of light horse.

In the meantime a rather more convenient and
comfortable litter had been devised out of a ladder
and a plank covered with cloaks and straw.   Upon
this the Duke was carried to Castelnaudary.
St Marie walked beside the litter and all the way
Montmorency supported himself by keeping his
right arm round the sergeant's neck. As the
litter passed through the ranks many of the soldiers
who had formerly served under Montmorency
hung their heads to conceal their emotion. They
seemed, says Du Cros, to be lamenting the misfortune of their general rather than their prisoner.[3]
A like emotion was displayed by the inhabitants

[1] Desormeaux, 405.   [2] Pontis, 180; Monlaur, 184.
[3] Du Cros, 263.

of Castelnaudary. When they arrived at the town Montmorency asked for water to be given him. The people standing round did not scruple to express their sympathy for him and with tears in their eyes assured him that he was in his own place. He was their Governor and they would obey no one else.[1] The attitude of the bystanders became so threatening that the six guards sent by Schomberg to escort the litter were obliged to draw their swords and threaten that they would use force if they were interfered with. The Duke himself was scarcely aware of what was happening around him, for he was so weak with loss of blood that he was rapidly sinking into unconsciousness.

The lodging prepared for the wounded Duke at Castelnaudary was that which had been occupied by the King the last time he had passed that way. Boutillon undressed the Duke and put him to bed and shortly after Schomberg's own surgeon arrived to dress his wounds. But Montmorency said that he did not know him and would not allow him to touch his wounds. The surgeon was most indignant and protested in vain that he belonged to the King. Montmorency would not have his wounds touched until his own surgeon, Lucante, arrived. Lucante was deeply attached to his master and when he first saw him was so overcome with distress that he gave way to his grief instead of

[1] Desormeaux, 396.

attending to the wounds. With some humour
Montmorency turned to him and said: "Lucante,
do not afflict me; but if you hope to be able to
help me do it at once, otherwise let me die in
peace."[1] When he had examined the Duke,
Lucante said: "Courage, Monsieur, by the grace
of God you have no wounds that are dangerous."
"My friend," replied Montmorency, "you are mis-
taken, there is not one of them, not even the least,
which is not mortal."[2] The Duke was speaking
figuratively; but in truth his wounds were actually
so serious that it was hardly expected that he
would survive them. In all he had received
seventeen wounds. Five balls were still embedded
in his body, while those which had passed through,
in addition to his sword-wounds, had made no less
than twenty-four holes in his flesh. The gravest
wound was that in the throat.[3]

After his wounds had been dressed Montmorency
felt somewhat easier and began to discuss the
battle with Boutillon, to whom he said that if his
men had only followed him he would have made
a fine breach in the ranks of the royal forces. To
this Boutillon replied: "Yes, if you had had with
you those who were with you at Veillane, who this
time were against you." Montmorency seems to
have liked talking to these old soldiers, many of

[1] Du Cros, 264.   [2] Pitaval, 211.
[3] Du Cros, 265.

whom had formerly served under him. He often
sent for St Marie, who had returned to him his ring
and his buff leather collar. The Duke contemplated giving him the collar as a memento of the
battle, but it had been pierced in so many places
when he was wounded that he said that he must
give him something else. St Marie answered that
he expected no reward but from the King.

The Duke was treated with the utmost courtesy
and consideration while he was at Castelnaudary.
His trusty Captain of the Guards, Soudeilles, was
allowed to visit him,[1] and he was also permitted by
Schomberg to receive Naugas, Lieutenant of the
Duc d'Épernon's guards, who had been sent by
that Duke to assure Montmorency of his continued friendship and to promise that he would do
all in his power to intercede for him with the King.
Montmorency was so touched by Épernon's friendly
expression of sympathy at a time when to display
such a virtue might render him liable to suspicion
himself that he insisted upon writing to him at
once with his own hand, though he was very weak
and so rolled up in bandages that he could scarcely
move.[2]

The officers who had taken part in the Duke's
capture also came to pay their respects to him.
To two of them, Guitaut and St. Preuil, he said:

[1] Richelieu, *Mémoires* (Mich et Pouj) VIII, 409.
[2] *Life of Épernon,* 497.

"My friends, I have sacrificed myself for ingrates and cowards. I have recognized them as such ever since the siege of Beaucaire, and if I had had enough strength and prudence to profit by the warnings I was given then that I was being betrayed in the Duc d'Orléans' army, I should have avoided the misfortune into which I have fallen."[1]

This bitterness was justified. Neither at the battle nor afterwards had any attempt been made to save Montmorency. As soon as he was captured the Orléanist forces had abandoned the fight. As Richelieu himself put it: "The rest of Monsieur's army retired without fighting as if it had been struck by lightning at the Duke's capture."[2]   And this in spite of the fact that Gaston is reported to have declared that he would rather lose himself and all his army than abandon a person who was so dear to him as his cousin, the Duc de Montmorency.[3] He knew well enough that it was only through Montmorency that he had received any support in Languedoc and that his removal would mean the collapse of the whole rising. But he took the news calmly enough. When he was told of Montmorency's capture he simply whistled and quietly remarked: "Then all is lost."[4] The Comte de Brion and his following among Gaston's

[1] Pitaval, 197.
[2] Richelieu, *Mémoires* (Mich et Pouj) VIII, 409.
[3] Desormeaux, 394.
[4] Desormeaux, 393.

advisers did their utmost to persuade him to make
an attempt to rescue Montmorency at all costs,
but they were opposed by the Duc d'Elbeuf, who
successfully urged that such a course would be useless and dangerous. But there can be little doubt
that if Gaston had possessed courage and initiative
he could still have saved Montmorency. His
numbers were superior to those of Schomberg and
he could have invested Castelnaudary and forced
it to surrender by cutting the aqueduct that supplied the town with water.[1] The inhabitants were
already favourable to Montmorency and could have
been relied upon not to give Schomberg any support.
There should have been no difficulty in taking the
town before La Force could arrive, for to get there
he would have had to pass by way of Béziers which
still held for Gaston. It was because Schomberg
himself was of the opinion that Castelnaudary was
not strong enough to withstand a siege should
Monsieur venture to attack it that he decided that
Montmorency should be sent elsewhere.

It was not easy to decide where to send him.
Carcassonne was rejected as being too near the
Spanish frontier and Toulouse because Schomberg
was advised that attempts might be made to rescue
him on the way or even when he was there.[2] The
town was full of his supporters, and the authorities
frankly stated that they could not undertake to

[1] *Ibid*, 394.   [2] *Ibid*, 398.

guard him safely themselves and that they would not
consent to receive a garrison of 800 troops which
Schomberg proposed to provide for that purpose.[1]
In the end it was decided to send him to the castle
of Lectoure to await the King's orders. In spite
of his surgeon's vehement protests that he was not
in a condition to be moved at all while he was
still in the throes of a high fever, Schomberg gave
orders for him to start on September the 5th.[2]
Schomberg was neither harsh nor unkindly; it was
the consciousness of his grave responsibility that
made him order this dangerous journey for a man
who for five days had been lying between life and
death. He felt that he was surrounded by men
who, if they would not actively assist in Montmorency's escape, would deliberately look the
other way if an attempt were made. For this
reason he wrote to the King asking him to send a
Lieutenant of his own Guards and a dozen archers
to take over the task of guarding Montmorency.
Pending their arrival he would have him guarded
by some of his own household whom he could
trust implicitly, since there was too much sympathy for Montmorency in the army for him to
rely on ordinary guards.[3]

[1] *Mercure*, 1632, XVIII, 581.
[2] Rénée, 135.
[3] Richelieu, *Mémoires* (Mich et Pouj) VIII, 409.

CHAPTER X

Montmorency removed to Lectoure—The Duchess
receives news of his capture—The Duke's letter to her
—Plan to effect Montmorency's escape at St. Jory—
Gaston takes the Duchess to Olonzac—Her efforts to
save her husband—The King and Cardinal proceed to
Languedoc—Richelieu resolved on Montmorency's death
—Gaston signs an ignominious peace—Richelieu's speech
at the Council—Decision to try Montmorency at
Toulouse—The Duke at Lectoure—Attempts at escape
frustrated—Montmorency resigned to his fate—The
Court arrives at Toulouse—Intercessions for Montmorency—The Princesse de Guéménée approaches the
Cardinal—Views of Condé and Épernon—Montmorency's
family forbidden to approach Toulouse—The Princesse
de Condé makes the journey nevertheless—She is forbidden to enter the city—The Marquis de Brézé sent
to fetch Montmorency—Departure from Lectoure—
Entry into Toulouse—Arrival at the Hôtel de Ville—
A painful incident—Grief in Languedoc—The attitude
of the Church—The cries of the populace.

On September the 5th Schomberg's aide-de-
camp, De L'Isle, came to inform Montmorency
that it had been decided to transport him immediately to Lectoure. As the Duke was still very
weak and his wounds gave him a great deal of
pain, he ventured a protest, to which De L'Isle
replied with threats to use force to make him leave
his bed if he would not rise of his own accord. For

a moment Montmorency showed a gleam of anger, and, starting up in his bed, demanded his sword. But soon, recognizing the futility of resistance, he controlled himself and suffered himself to be dressed and carried to the litter which was awaiting him.[1]

It was some days before tidings of the defeat at Castelnaudary were brought to the Duchesse de Montmorency who had been waiting anxiously at Béziers. When the terrible truth was broken to her she fainted away. Prostrate with grief though she was, her first thought was for her husband's welfare, and she hastily despatched to him her own doctor and her squire, Maurens, who, on the day he left Castelnaudary, came to him at Villefranche, where a halt had been made in order that his wounds might be dressed.[2] Montmorency decided to send Maurens back to his wife. "You will inform your mistress," he said, "of the number and extent of my wounds which you have seen, and you will assure her that the wound I have inflicted on her heart pains me a thousand times more than all the others." He also sent her a letter written with his own hand.[3]

"My heart, I have received singular consolation in seeing Maurens. I had already written to you

---

[1] Du Cros, 265.   [2] *Ibid*, 266–7.
[3] According to Monlaur the original letter is preserved in the Convent of the Visitation at Moulins.

what they thought of my wounds. I assure you
that they are as he will inform you, and that the
most poignant pain I feel in my misfortunes is the
imagination of your sufferings. Banish them for
love of me, I beg of you, since my life is safe
and God does everything for the best. Goodbye,
I am all yours.

"MONTMORENCY."

At St Jory another halt was made for the night
at a house by the roadside. The mistress of the
house planned to effect Montmorency's escape by
means of a secret passage which ran from his bedchamber down to the cellars, and it is said that
the guards themselves were ready to wink at his
escape if not even to afford active assistance; but
it was found impossible to carry out the project
owing to the Duke's extreme weakness, for he
fainted every time he attempted to move. It was
therefore judged inexpedient to endeavour any
further attempts at rescue until after he had
reached Lectoure and had had some time to recu-
perate.[1]

With the defeat at Castelnaudary and the capture
of Montmorency the Orléanist forces had melted
away, and Gaston himself with a few faithful
followers had retired from Alzonne to Béziers.
On September the 21st he received the news that
Schomberg was approaching the town, and forth-

[1] Du Cros, 267.

with caused the Duchess, ill though she was, to be placed in a litter and carried off to Olonzac.[1] He swore to her that he would never abandon her husband and would insist on his pardon as the one indispensable condition of the terms he was about to make with the King.[2]

At Olonzac Marie Félice was to her astonishment informed that her flight with Gaston had been construed as a further act of rebellion, that her husband's misfortunes were attributed solely to her own evil counsels, and that it was even proposed to bring her also to trial.[3] In spite of her illness she determined forthwith to return to Béziers. This she was not permitted to do; she received the King's order to retire instead to La Grange des Prés. Even at Pézénas she found that the Duke's misfortunes were set down to her so that all the townsfolk shunned her.[4]

Marie Félice left no stone unturned to help her husband. She sent Maurens to the Condés, the Angoulêmes, and the Ventadours, begging them to rally to his support, and wrote letters to all his friends and even to his enemies imploring them to intercede for him with the King. It was by her influence that all the towns and fortified places in Languedoc that still held out against the King made their submission.[5] Finally she sent Sou-

---

[1] *Mercure*, 1632, XVIII, 770.   [3] *Ibid.*
[2] Du Cros, 272.   [4] Cotolendi, 57; Monlaur, 189
            [5] Du Cros, 269.

deilles, the Captain of Montmorency's guards and
the only one of his followers who had warned him
against rebellion, to the King to request that she
might be allowed to come and throw herself at his
feet in supplication. On his return from this
mission he was obliged to tell her that the King
would not listen to any of her offers and formally
forbade her to approach him.[1]

For one moment there came into her despairing
brain the mad project of flying from France by sea
and afterwards giving out that she had been shipwrecked and drowned, in the hope that the ambitious Cardinal would pardon her husband so that
he could marry him to one of his own relations
and thus clip his wings. The only expedient she
would not try was that of magic, and when certain
wise women came to her proposing to save the
Duke by occult means she flatly refused to listen
to their ungodly counsels.[2]

From the time when the rebellion had started
Richelieu had represented to the King the importance of going to Languedoc in person as soon as it
had been suppressed in order to reap the fruits of
his victory over the province which had so stub-
bornly resisted the extension of the royal authority
over it. When the news of the battle of Castelnaudary was brought to the Court at Lyons
Richelieu resolved to proceed at once to Languedoc

[1] Du Cros, 269.   [2] Cotolendi, 52–4.

and bring Montmorency to trial.   There seems little
doubt that Richelieu was already firmly determined on Montmorency's death and had welcomed
the rebellion for this reason, if, indeed, he can be
absolved of having in some measure engineered
the whole thing from the beginning with this very
object.   Certain it is that he had forced Montmorency to go on with the rebellion after his
repeated offers to withdraw on what were far from
being unreasonable conditions.

When at first it seemed likely that Montmorency
would die of his wounds, the Cardinal, who was
anxious only for his removal by no matter what
means, affected to feel deeply sorry for him, but
he changed his mind as soon as it was known that
he was recovering.[1]   It is said that he made the
most of the incident of the discovery of the Queen's
portrait to arouse Louis XIII's jealousy against
Montmorency and to keep him vindictively inclined.   Possibly there was also a spark of jealousy
on his own account, since he too had aspired to the
Queen's favours without success.

Louis XIII was quite prepared to forgive his
brother and the Cardinal also was ready to receive
the erring sheep back into the fold provided that
the Duc de Montmorency were not allowed to
return with him.   The King sent Aiguebonne to
Gaston to inform him that a request for pardon on

[1] Rénée, 136.

his part would be acceded to on reasonable conditions. Gaston had not even awaited the King's move, but had already despatched to him a messenger who, curiously enough, was Aiguebonne's brother, Chaudebonne. Gaston set forth two indispensable conditions without which he affirmed he could never make peace. The first was that the Duc de Montmorency should be restored to liberty and should be confirmed in all his honours, dignities, and possessions, the second, that the like immunity from punishment should be conceded to all his own followers and those of the Queen-Mother. The second demand was granted readily enough, but to the first the King and the Cardinal returned a flat refusal.[1] Gaston once more sent the Comte de Brion to beg for Montmorency's life, but the refusal was persisted in.[2] Brion, however, was of opinion from what he had seen at Court that there was genuine anxiety there for peace and that if Gaston remained firm his request would in the end be reluctantly granted. But the emissaries of the Cardinal had by this time succeeded in convincing Gaston that he would never gain his own pardon except by abandoning Montmorency, and he was pusillanimous enough to depart from his solemn word in order to save his own skin. He signed a most ignominious treaty

[1] Goulas, I, 193; *Mémoire donné à M. D'Aiguebonne etc*; *Mercure*, 1632, XVIII, 763.
[2] *Mercure*, 1632, XVIII, 772.

PLATE VII

LVDOVICVS XIII BORBONIVS
D.G.FRANCIÆ ET NAVARRÆ
REX CHRISTIANISSIMVS.

face p. 212

by which he basely agreed to interest himself no
further in any of those who had been joined with
him in this enterprise and to refrain from making
any complaints regarding the punishment the King
might think fit to inflict on them.   In addition, he
pledged himself henceforth to love the Cardinal![1]

Richelieu was so determined upon Montmorency's
death that he was prepared, if necessary, to dis-
pense with all legal formalities.   An ordinance was
actually prepared and sealed providing for his
decapitation without trial.[2]   But when Gaston
incontinently abandoned his friend so that he
ceased to be an important piece in the game of
negotiation, the Cardinal came to consider that it
might be desirable that a certain parade of justice
with some semblance of legality should attend his
inevitable condemnation, and therefore requested
the King to summon his Council and take its advice
in the matter.   He himself took charge of the proceedings and made a long and insidious speech.[3]
He began by expressing his heartfelt pity for Montmorency in his misfortunes and extolled the great
and manifold services to the State of his ancestors,
his father, and himself.   He then affected to weigh
with scrupulous care the various reasons for and
against clemency.   In the end he came to what
he affirmed was the reluctant conclusion that it

[1] *Mercure*, 1632, XVIII, 774–8.   [2] Aumale, III, 245.
[3] Desormeaux, 406.

would be impossible to pardon him. "There could be no security," he said, "in keeping in prison a man who is so considerable through his alliances. The Duc de Montmorency's party in Languedoc will fall with his head."[1]

The rest of the Council expressed themselves convinced by the Cardinal's eloquent arguments and the King himself concurred in the decision. Although Montmorency, as a peer, had an indisputable right to be tried only by the Parlement of Paris, it was arranged quite illegally that he should be tried by the Parlement of Toulouse. This decision was made by the Cardinal, who took a fiendish satisfaction in the thought that he would be disgraced in the midst of his own government and among the people who most held him in honour.[2] Moreover, he appears to have considered that the local Parlement could be more easily influenced and overawed. In order to ensure this he suggested that the King and he should proceed to Toulouse to lend the weight of their presence. The president of the Court was to be the Chancellor, Châteauneuf, who, although he had been one of Montmorency's childhood friends when a page to his father, the Constable, was now a creature of the Cardinal's and devoted to his interests.

In the meantime Montmorency was being kept in honourable though close confinement at Lec-

---

[1] Rénée, 137.   [2] Pontis, 181.

toure. His own physician, surgeon, and apothecary shared his imprisonment in order that they might attend on him,[1] but all others of his friends were denied access to him, though it is said that all the time he was at Lectoure Marie Félice contrived to send him messages by couriers who knew full well that every time they undertook the journey they were risking their lives.[2]

Schomberg was very anxious to shift the responsibility of guarding Montmorency on to the King himself, and continued to write asking for special guards, since so great was Montmorency's popularity with all ranks of the army that he could not be sure even of his own Captain of the Guards, La Jaille, and ten picked men whom he had sent to Lectoure in addition to the ordinary garrison.[3]

Various attempts made by Montmorency's friends to effect his escape proved that the Marshal's anxiety was not ill founded. The greatest obstacle in the way of these attempts was that, at any rate at the beginning of his imprisonment, the Duke was too weak to move.[4] The most spectacular attempt was that engineered by a lady of gallant and adventurous disposition, a certain Madame de Castelnau. One of the sentries was bribed to smuggle through a

[1] Richelieu, *Mémoires* (Mich et Pouj) VIII, 409.
[2] Monlaur, 187.
[3] Richelieu, *Mémoires*, VIII, 409.
[4] Desormeaux, 398.

bundle of silken cords by means of which it was intended that the Duke should cross the walls and gain the open country, where the lady would be awaiting him with an escort of twenty trusty cavaliers. Unfortunately the plot was frustrated by one of the officers of the garrison, who caught the sentry red-handed with the ropes and slew him on the spot.[1] It is also related that the commander of the garrison, a member of the Puységur family, was offered a sum of two hundred thousand livres if he would contrive or even connive at the Duke's escape, but that, in spite of his friendliness for Montmorency and although the offer was increased, he refused to commit this breach of trust.[2]

When Montmorency heard that the King and the Cardinal were coming to Languedoc and that he was to be brought to trial, he knew that his fate was already settled. He did not attempt to conceal from himself that the result of the trial could only be a sentence of death. One day as he was gazing out of the window he saw a group of workers in the vineyards celebrating the vendange, and his face lit up with pleasure at the familiar scene. His doctor was astonished at his lightheartedness. "Is it possible, Monsieur," he said, "that, being so near to and so certain of your doom, you think of it so lightly?" Montmorency replied simply that the thought of it did not trouble his peace of mind.

[1] Pitaval, 212.   [2] Puységur, I, 129.

' But how do you know that they will not compass
your death here?'" went on the doctor. "All the
better," said Montmorency with a laugh, "it would
save me the trouble of going to Toulouse."[1] He
had evidently become quite resigned to the thought
of his approaching death, and while he was at
Lectoure even caused a white suit to be made for
him in which to go to his execution.[2]

When the Court reached Béziers on the 6th of
October the Estates were held and the Archbishop
of Narbonne delivered an eloquent plea to the King
to temper his justice with mercy. On the 14th the
King and the Cardinal left for Toulouse and passed
by way of Castelnaudary, where they paid a visit to
the battlefield. On the 22nd they arrived at
Toulouse.[3]

From the moment that the news of Montmorency's capture had become known the King
and the Cardinal had been besieged by appeals
from all quarters to show him clemency. Even
before the Court left Lyons the Princesse de
Guéménée was actually bold enough to seek the
Cardinal and remind him of all that he owed to
Montmorency. "Madame," said Richelieu coldly,
"I was not the first to break off the friendship."[4]
As was only natural, Montmorency's own relations
were foremost in endeavouring to help him. Condé

[1] Du Cros, 277–8; Desormeaux, 415.   [3] Mercure, 1632, XVIII, 815.
[2] Du Cros, 277.   [4] Desormeaux, 399.

with characteristic pride of race was quite confident that Montmorency would be pardoned in view of his rank and services and also of his relationship with his august self.[1] Nevertheless, he thought it best to consult the Duc d'Épernon, who was emphatic that everything possible should be done to save a man so necessary to France. But Épernon did not share Condé's belief that he would be pardoned. 'He gave him at the first for lost,' says his biographer, 'and being very well acquainted with the severe maxims of that time, together with the implacable hatred the great Minister had conceived against him, did forthwith conclude, that this first offence would also be the last he was ever likely to commit.'[2]

Richelieu deemed it advisable to take steps to prevent any of Montmorency's family from approaching Toulouse. The Duc de Ventadour was the only one of them who was already there and on the arrival of the Court he was ordered to leave the town at once.[3] Montmorency's step-mother, the Constabless, and the Duchesse d'Angoulême, who had started for Toulouse, were stopped at Cahors by the King's orders.[4] Condé was instructed to remain at Bourges, while the Duc d'Angoulême and the Duchesse de Ventadour were forbidden to leave Paris. All of them did what

[1] *Ibid.* 410.   [3] Du Cros, 274; *Mercure*, XVIII, 816.
[2] *Life of Épernon*, 497.   [4] Desormeaux, 413.

they could by writing to the King and the Cardinal, offering their own children as hostages for Montmorency's good behaviour if he were pardoned.

Whether Montmorency's favourite sister, the Princesse de Condé, had received no order to remain in Paris or whether she had received it and disobeyed it, at all events she hastened towards Toulouse with the design of interceding with the King and the Cardinal in person. Undeterred by the floods which hampered her progress she journeyed night and day, but when she came near Toulouse she was met by a messenger from the King forbidding her to enter the city.[1] This prohibition was due to Richelieu, who was determined at all costs to prevent her from seeing the King. The messenger, one Saugain, happening to be an old servant of hers, the Princess wept on his shoulder and, in the hope of exciting the royal compassion, told him to go back and inform the King of the state she was in. When Saugain returned he bore a message from the Chancellor Châteauneuf bidding her return home. All the Princess's angry pride was aroused by this message; she haughtily replied that a person of her rank received orders only from the King himself and that she refused to go away. Louis thereupon sent her a formal order forbidding her to enter the

[1] *Ibid*, 414.

city.[1] This she could not venture to disobey, so, seeing that it was impossible for her to enter Toulouse, she decided to remain at the Château de Creuzel, not far from the city. When her request for an interview with her brother was also refused, she caused a memorandum for his defence to be prepared and sent to him. The Duke, who received it on his way to Toulouse, was extremely touched, but said that he was resolved not to wrangle about his life, and tore it up.[2]

A few days after the Court had arrived at Toulouse the Marquis de Brezé was sent with an escort of cavalry to conduct Montmorency from Lectoure. The Duke received him courteously, enquiring after the health of the King and the Cardinal and intimating that he would be ready to start almost immediately, if he might have time to have his wounds dressed again before leaving.[3]

It was a magnificent September day when Montmorency left Lectoure. He was seated in a carriage with Brezé, and eight companies of light horse rode with them ready to prevent any attempt at rescue or escape. Among the gentlemen who rode beside the carriage were the Baron de Laurières and Beauregard, both of whom had been wounded by Montmorency at Castelnaudary. Beauregard still carried his arm in a sling.[4] The Duke whiled

---

[1] Aumale, III, 248.
[2] Du Cros, 278; Desormeaux, 416.
[3] Du Cros, 278.
[4] Ibid.

away the time by discussing the battle with them. When they reached the outskirts of the town about midday on October the 27th, Brezé descended and caused the carriage to be closed so that the prisoner would no longer be visible.[1] As the carriage entered the town it was completely surrounded by footguards and as an additional precaution the streets through which it passed were lined by a double row of Swiss guards.

The populace made no attempt to conceal their grief and a cry of pity went up as Montmorency descended from the carriage at the Hôtel de Ville, where he was to be lodged under the care of Launay, Lieutenant of the Guards. According to one account the Duke's eyes were bandaged,[2] but this cannot have been so if there is any truth in another story which relates that as he alighted a sinister sight greeted his eyes. The corpses of two officers who had killed each other in a duel were dragged past on hurdles with halters round their necks on their way to the Place St Georges, where they were to be hanged by the feet. Montmorency is said to have recognized them both as former companions in arms.[3]

The first impulse of ingratitude to Montmorency in Languedoc had probably been inspired merely by fear, for by now sentiment had veered round

[1] *Mercure*, 1632, XVIII, 820.   [2] Monlaur, 191.
[3] Puységur, I, 130; *Mercure*, 1632, XVIII, 818; Rénée, 139.

completely and piteous murmurs arose from all over the province. "Let them deprive us of our liberties," cried the people of Languedoc, "let them take away our goods and our children, let them kill us all, but let them spare his life."[1] These deep feelings were further encouraged by the Church, led by Cardinal de la Valette, whose influence was considerable in the town where he had once been Archbishop. He caused the sacrament to be exposed in all the churches and prayers to be said on Montmorency's behalf at services which he himself and many of the nobility attended. His example was followed by all the other bishops in Languedoc. In all the towns there were public processions as on days of mourning and calamity and in Toulouse the blue penitents made solemn pilgrimage to the relics of St Simon and St Jude and dedicated their devotions as an intercession for Montmorency.[2] The populace gave vent to their feelings even more openly. The King could not go out of doors without having his ears assailed with cries of "Grâce! Grâce! Miséricorde!"

[1] Du Cros, 275; Baillon, 176.   [2] Pontis, 182.

CHAPTER XI

Montmorency's trial a mere formality—Troops poured into Toulouse—Montmorency interrogated by commissioners—Confrontation of witnesses—The Duke's anger with Guilleminet—Father Arnoux—Montmorency's last speeches—He makes his confession and sets his worldly affairs in order—His last letter to Marie Félice—Richelieu agrees to visit the Princesse de Condé—His hypocrisy at the interview—The Duc d'Épernon approaches the King—The nobility intercede for Montmorency—Gaston's messenger—St. Preuil and Châtelet—Grief of the people of Toulouse—Montmorency escorted to the Parlement—His demeanour at the trial—His condemnation—Emotion of the judges—The King sends for Launay—Montmorency consoles his guards—Charlus comes to demand the insignia of his orders—The Duke's last preparations—He hears his sentence read—His last conversation with Arnoux—The place of execution changed at the last moment—Montmorency goes to his death—The last scenes—The body removed for burial—All Languedoc in mourning—An ode on Montmorency's death—Consternation of the nobility—The Cardinal responsible for the Duke's execution—Louis XIII's subsequent regret—The shame of Gaston d'Orléans—The news of her husband's death broken to the Duchess.

That the Duc de Montmorency's trial was to be a mere formality and could have but one result

Note.—The chief authorities from which the narrative in this chapter has been derived are dealt with at length in the Bibliographica Appendix, p. 269. The footnotes refer merely to additional sources or are concerned with special points.

was known to both accusers and accused. The preparations for the execution were made even before the trial. It was, of course, already notorious that Montmorency did not intend to defend himself, partly because he recognized his guilt and in his own mind had decided that he merited death, partly because he knew the Cardinal too well to imagine that it was worth while either to defend himself, or, confessing his guilt, to sue for pardon.

Richelieu had long ago resolved that Montmorency should die, and was not prepared to take any risks. The city of Toulouse was overawed by a display of military force. Immediately upon the King's arrival the gates of the town had been closed and the keys handed over to His Majesty. During the following days some eight thousand troops were brought into the town ready to act on the slightest sign of any disturbance.[1] Precautions were taken to prevent any attempt at escape on the part of Montmorency. His room at the Hôtel de Ville had been specially prepared against his coming. The windows were heavily barred, extra bolts were placed on the doors, and a grating was set in the chimney so that there should be no egress by that way.[2]

An hour or so after Montmorency's arrival in Toulouse two commissioners, Anne de Cadillac and Clément du Lonc, came to interrogate him and at

---

[1] Pontis, 183.   [2] Desormeaux, 417.

the same time to inform him officially of the decision
to have him tried by the Parlement of Toulouse.
The Duke made answer to them: "Messieurs, I
could claim that in my quality of Duke and Peer
I cannot and ought not to be judged except by the
Parlement of Paris; but my crime is of such a
nature that, if the King does not pardon me, there
is no judge in his kingdom who would not have
power to condemn me; and so, since His Majesty
commands it, I will obey, though my submission
may cost me my life." He also declared that he
was pleased that he was to be tried by the Parlement of Toulouse, since he had always regarded its
members as worthy men.

On the following day, October 28th, the interrogatory was continued and Montmorency was con-
fronted with the officers and soldiers who had taken
him prisoner at Castelnaudary. There were seven
of them in all, the two sergeants, St Marie and
Boutillon, and five officers, Guitaut, Beauregard,
Savignac, Espénan, and St. Preuil. The Duke received them all courteously, rather as friends than
as hostile witnesses; and, indeed, they were all to
a man reluctant to give testimony against him.
Most of them were personally known to him, and
Boutillon, if not several of the others also, had
actually served under him. All gave their evidence
simply and straightforwardly and as much in favour
of the accused as possible.

Q

Montmorency was deeply touched by their attitude. While one of them was giving evidence, he turned to St. Preuil and remarked: "Look at poor Guitaut: I believe he will do nothing but weep when he has to speak." Guitaut, in fact, could hardly restrain his emotion when he related how he had not recognized Monsieur de Montmorency at first owing to the fire and smoke of the battle which had enveloped him, but that when he had seen him break through six of their ranks and kill soldiers in the seventh he had realized that it could be no one else. The Duke thereupon smilingly protested that Guitaut was doing him too much honour.

The evidence of Guilleminet, the registrar of the Estates, was less reluctant, or so at least Montmorency thought, being of the opinion that he came of his own accord to bear witness against him. It is more likely that he was simply eager to justify himself, since his own position was somewhat precarious. He declared that in the matter of countersigning the commissions he had been coerced by the Duke, who, when he had hesitated or refused to sign his name, had angrily said to him: "Hurry up, you are a babbler." As soon as he had been able to withdraw into safety he had promptly disavowed his actions as being done under constraint. Montmorency was most indignant at his evidence and accused him of being a scoundrel and a forger.

The Princesse de Condé, anxious that her brother should not be deprived of spiritual help at this time, had asked Cardinal de la Valette to endeavour to secure permission for him to be attended by a confessor.[1] The Cardinal approached Richelieu, who referred him to the Chancellor. But Châteauneuf refused to grant the request ; he declared that Montmorency must be treated as a criminal and could not be allowed to have a confessor until sentence had been passed on him. On hearing this harsh decision Richelieu had the decency to intervene and gave orders that the Duke was not to be treated as a common criminal and that the Jesuit father, Arnoux, was to be sent to him. Montmorency had himself asked for Arnoux, for whom he had always had the greatest respect.

When the Jesuit arrived at seven o'clock in the evening Montmorency greeted him with joy. "Father," he said, "I pray you to place me at this very hour on the shortest and surest way to Heaven that you know, for I have nothing more to hope for or wish for but God." He informed Arnoux that he would need half the next day to make his general confession and take the sacrament, and Launay readily undertook to endeavour to obtain this boon for him from the King. At the same time he asked if the Duke would permit him to carry a message from him suing for pardon. After

[1] Desormeaux, 425–6.

consulting the priest Montmorency told him that he might inform the Cardinal that, should he think fit to show him mercy, he would never have any cause to regret having done so, but that, if his death were thought necessary for the good of the State, he was ready and willing to die.

Montmorency spent most of the following night in prayer, and when Arnoux arrived at six o'clock the next morning he found him already out of bed. "This is a great day," said the Duke, "I have need of God's succour and your assistance, the more so as I feel myself unworthy of the mercy he has shown me in giving me so great a contempt for death. It is such, Father, that I must beg you to take care that I am not carried away by vanity in the matter. Feel whether my heart is beating or my pulse going faster than usual, and you will agree with me that it is God alone who is giving me strength and delivering me from the horrors of death. I know that without him my misfortune is so great that I should falter like another in my resolution."

It is difficult to reconcile the last speeches of the Duke with the accounts of him as a man devoid of wit or eloquence given by Tallemant des Réaux and others. Yet his words are recorded by contemporary authorities, and there can be little doubt that they are substantially correct. Du Cros, indeed, goes out of his way to explain that

the reports of the Duke's last speeches are
authentic. 'Here then,' he says, 'I shall quit the
rôle of historian to take up that of secretary, and
shall report a part of the discourses of this great
man as they came to my knowledge.'[1] In all
probability the sentiments at least are Montmorency's, even if the actual form of the words
may have been edited and improved. At any
rate Arnoux professed himself deeply affected by
Montmorency's conduct, and afterwards declared
that he would esteem himself blessed if God permitted him to die with a resignation such as was
shown by Montmorency during his last days, and
that, in the short time he had assisted him, he
himself had learnt better how to die than in all the
meditations of his life.[2]

After his wounds had been attended to the Duke
dressed himself. Arnoux persuaded him to substi-
tute a holy reliquary for the jewelled bracelet he
had hitherto worn. Montmorency was under the
impression that he was to be executed that very
day and welcomed the thought that it was a Friday
so that he would meet his death on the same day
of the week as Jesus Christ. Owing to the pain
from his wounds he had some difficulty in getting
to a kneeling posture to make his general confession. But in spite of his sufferings he remained
on his knees for two hours confessing his sins with

[1] Du Cros, 287.   [2] Pitaval, 258-9.

many tears and expressions of regret and repentance. When at length he received absolution he cried: "I no longer want to live; I desire no delays and shall be sorry if there are any. How good God is and how I hope to see him soon!" After his confession he was escorted to the Chapel to hear Mass. When he had communicated he said to Father Arnoux: "He who has within him the Author of Life no longer fears death. I hope soon to see God whom I have just received in the sacrament."

Montmorency received with indifference, even with regret, the news that his execution had been put off for a day which Launay brought him on his return from the Chapel. He spent the rest of the morning in prayers and conversation with his confessor, but in the afternoon he turned his attention to settling his worldly affairs. Although all his property had been declared confiscated, the King desired him to put on paper his last wishes regarding its disposal so that he might follow them if he felt so inclined. The Duke wrote to Cardinal de la Valette confiding his body-servant to him, and asking him for a hundred pistoles to give to his surgeon. He also wrote an affectionate letter to the Princesse de Condé. Afterwards he made his will, which he gave to St Preuil to deliver to the King, instructing him also to inform the Cardinal that he was presenting him with one of his most valuable pictures, a 'Martyrdom of St Sebastian' by Caraccio, to show him that he died his humble servant. This was a gesture characteristic of Montmorency, and it cannot be denied that the subject was entirely appropriate.[1]

When he had made all his other dispositions the Duke sat down to compose his last letter to Marie Félice.

'My dear heart, I say the last farewell to you with the same affection that has always existed between us. I implore you by the peace of my soul which I hope will soon be in Heaven, to moderate your grief and receive this affliction from the hand of our sweet Saviour. I am receiving so much grace from his goodness that you should have every reason for finding consolation. Farewell, once more, my dear heart, farewell.'

From the Château de Creuzel the Princesse de Condé had not ceased her supplications to the King and the Cardinal. After repeated requests Richelieu at length consented to grant her an interview at the Château. Fearing that some attempt might be made on him there by way of reprisal,

---

[1] Some accounts (my own MS, the *Histoire Véritable*, and Pontis) declare that the picture represented St. Francis, but all the others (*Mercure François*, Mazarin MS, Du Cros, Desormeaux, Rénée, Baillon, Monlaur, and Pitaval) have St. Sebastian. It is Desormeaux who gives the name of the painter. Rénée, on the authority of Sauval's *Antiquités de Paris* adds that Montmorency also gave the Cardinal two superb marble statues, 'Les Deux Captifs' by Michael Angelo from the Château of Ecouen. They are now in the Louvre.

he sent to spy out the land before he would proceed
to the meeting-place. As soon as he entered the
room Charlotte de Condé threw herself at his feet
with prayers and tears. The Cardinal's ready
hypocrisy did not desert him; he too fell on his
knees beside her and mingled his crocodile tears
with her sincere ones, promising that he would do
all in his power to move the King to clemency.
He assured her at the same time that the best way
in which she could ensure obtaining the King's
mercy would be to withdraw herself from the
neighbourhood of Toulouse.[1]

While the Princesse de Condé was pleading with
the Cardinal, the Duc d'Épernon had sought the
King with the same object. Although eighty
years old and now very feeble, he had made a
special journey from Bordeaux to beg the King's
clemency. He had promised both Marie Félice
and Condé that he would do his utmost to save
Montmorency, whom he himself had always held
in very genuine affection. His plea should have
carried all the more weight in that from the very
beginning of the revolt he had, to the great relief
of the Court, denounced it and declared his loyalty
to the Crown. Moreover, he used the very sound
argument that in former days both he himself and
the Cardinal had been guilty of the same offence
and had been pardoned, and that the King had

[1] Desormeaux, 422–5; Rénée, 152–3.

never had any cause to regret having exercised his prerogative of mercy on their behalf. But with all his eloquence he could make no impression on Louis XIII, who with his eyes fixed on the ground remained plunged in gloomy silence, and finally, perceiving that his mission was hopeless, he asked leave to retire to his own government that he might not be present in the city at the time of his friend's death. "Yes, you have free leave," said the King, adding with sinister import," neither do I intend myself to stay long in this city." Sadly Épernon left Toulouse and passed by the Château de Creuzel to inform the Princesse de Condé of his failure. As he arrived he met Richelieu coming away. Both he and the Princess now realized that there was no further hope.[1]

The King and the Cardinal were almost alone in desiring Montmorency's death. All the most illustrious persons at Court joined in the appeals for him, even some who in former days had had no cause to love him as, for instance, the Duc de Chevreuse. Another erstwhile enemy, the Duc de Retz, went with Montmorency's nephew, the Comte d'Alais, to intercede with the Cardinal. To them Richelieu made no secret of his hatred of Montmorency In the middle of their discourse he interrupted them rudely, saying that the Duc de Montmorency had become so insupportable and so jealous that he

---

[1] *Life of Épernon*, 499–501; Desormeaux, 421–2.

could not bear to see anyone above him.[1] Louis XIII's own favourite, the Duc de St Simon, grew so heated in his remonstrances with his royal master that he gave him deep offence and ran the risk of losing his favour. The victor of Castelnaudary, the Maréchal de Schomberg, came himself to plead for the man he had defeated. He requested to be allowed to decline the government of Languedoc which had been offered to him, affirming that he would not accept the government of a gentleman who was still alive and who, he hoped, might be able to ask it back from the King, if he were pardoned.

The ladies of the Court were particularly forward in their entreaties, for Montmorency had always been a favourite with them, Some of them sought the Queen and implored her to use her influence with her husband. But fearing lest she might be suspected of possessing too deep an interest in his fate she hesitated to do so and consulted Richelieu, who of course was careful to advise her that it would be sheer madness on her part to intervene.[2]

Even the Duc d'Orléans, the cause of all the trouble, managed, in spite of his promise not to interfere, to summon up sufficient courage to add his appeal. He realized that Montmorency was being made the scapegoat of the whole rebellion, since he himself and the Duc d'Elbeuf had been

---

[1] Desormeaux, 413.   [2] Desormeaux, 435; Pitaval, 229.

pardoned and he had been allowed to save many
of his other followers by claiming them as members
of his personal household, which had been granted
immunity by the treaty. No objection had been
made to this proceeding, though it was manifest
that his household could never have been so large
as it had suddenly become since the treaty. Goulas
remarks that a great deal of parchment and paper
was employed in hastily issuing forth commissions
as chamberlains to the members of the nobility and
gentry who had followed Monsieur on his ill-fated
venture.[1] On the evening of the 29th La Vaupot
came on Gaston's behalf to intercede with the King.
Though he was eloquent in his pleading and three
times threw himself on his knees in supplication at
the King's feet, Louis remained inexorable and
coldly informed the envoy that the matter was in
the hands of the Parlement.[2]

Perhaps the most touching appeal of all was that
made at great risk to himself by St Preuil, one of
the officers who had been instrumental in effecting
Montmorency's capture. Being no more than a
simple gentleman he had no right to add his prayers
to those of the great ones of the land. Nevertheless,
basing his claim on the fact that the Duke was his
prisoner, he had the extraordinary courage to
approach the King in the presence of the Cardinal.[3]

[1] Goulas, II, 198.   [2] Gonias, II, 205-6; Desormeaux, 434.
[3] Desormeaux, 431.

Louis XIII merely laughed at him and turned away.
St Preuil thereupon lost control of himself and said
that if he had been able to foresee the fate reserved
for the Duc de Montmorency, he would have shot
him instead of taking him prisoner. This temerity
infuriated Richelieu, who turned savagely on him
and said: "St Preuil, if the King served you right,
he would set your head where your heels stand."
Pontis, who was present on this occasion, remarks:
"I heard this compliment myself, which I confess
to me seemed something sparkish for a Bishop to
make."[1]

Another bold answer was made to the King by
Châtelet, Master of the Requests. Noticing his
gloom and divining the cause, Louis said to him:
"I believe you would have given your arm to save
Monsieur de Montmorency." "I would have given
both," he cried, "to save for you one which has
gained and would yet gain battles for you."[2]

It is said that representations on Montmorency's
behalf were also received from the Pope, the Queen
of England, the Duke of Savoy, who asked clemency
for the man who had defeated him at Veillane and
Carignan, and the Republic of Venice, which besought the King of France to allow it to have Montmorency to take command of the Venetian armies.
The messenger from England did not arrive till
after the Duke's execution, and it is obvious that

[1] Pontis, 183.   [2] Desormeaux, 432.

the others, even if they were sent as soon as the
news of his capture had spread abroad, must also
have come too late.[1]

The cries of the people of Toulouse never ceased
throughout these days; they thronged the street
outside the King's lodging calling for mercy for
their beloved Governor. One of the courtiers, some
say the Duc de Châtillon,[2] others the Marquis de
Brezé,[3] tried to enlist the King's sympathy by
drawing attention to the popular grief: "Sire, if
Your Majesty will look through the window, you
will take compassion on these poor people who are
imploring your clemency on behalf of Monsieur de
Montmorency." Louis XIII's reply was characteristic of him: "I should not be a king if I possessed
the feelings of the people and private individuals."

It having come to the ears of the Cardinal that
the students had sworn to snatch Montmorency
away even on the very steps of the scaffold,[4] on
the night of the 29th more troops were poured into
the town, making some twelve thousand in all.
Scarcely anyone in Toulouse slept that night save
the Duc de Montmorency himself. In the evening
he had received a visit from his faithful friend,
Cardinal de la Valette, who had remained with him
for an hour, and afterwards he had conversed for
some time with Father Arnoux. He seemed scarcely

[1] *Ibid*, 430–1.
[2] Desormeaux; Rénée.
[3] Pontis; *Mercure François*.
[4] Rénée, 151.

to show any sign that he was at all affected by the
thought of the dreadful fate which overhung him,
save once when he said to the priest: "Father,
this flesh would fain remember and complain, but
with God's grace we will prevent it." During
these last hours his thoughts turned most to Marie
Félice, and the imminence of his separation from
her seemed to grieve him more than anything
else. But the thought of her faith in God consoled him, for he felt that because of it the
blow of his death might strengthen instead of
weakening her.

For the greater part of the night he slept calmly
and peacefully, though he was once awakened by
the prayers of his surgeon who was kneeling beside
his bed. Montmorency called to him and said:
"Praised be God, who has thought fit to deliver me
from the anxiety into which the thought of the
perils I feared for my wife was continually driving
me, and to remit altogether to Providence the useless cares which I had. You will tell her that I
recommend two things to her: the first, to pardon
all my enemies willingly as I have done, the second,
to forgive the grief I may have caused her when we
were together." After this he fell again into so
profound and calm a sleep that Father Arnoux had
actually to awaken him on the last morning of his
life. *"Surgite, eamus,"* said Montmorency as he
rose. When his surgeon, Lucante, came to dress

his wounds for the last time the Duke remarked
gaily: "The time has come to heal all these wounds
with a single one."

Between seven and eight o'clock the Comte de
Charlus, Captain of the Royal Guards and a distant
kinsman of his own, arrived to escort him to his
trial. Accompanied by Charlus and Launay he
was driven down to the Parlement in a closed carriage. Every precaution had been taken to prevent
a demonstration of popular sympathy; the carriage
was surrounded by guards and the streets between
the Hôtel de Ville and the Parlement were lined
with troops.

When the Duc de Montmorency entered the court
his demeanour was as proud and majestic as it had
ever been in the days when he was Governor of
the province and presided over the Estates. In
deference to his rank he was not bound as prisoners
usually were, and the stool which had been provided for him was placed as high as the judges'
seats. When he was brought in there was scarce
one of the hundred judges who did not lower his
eyes unwilling to meet his gaze, and many held
their handkerchiefs to their faces to conceal their
emotion.

Montmorency had already decided to make no
attempt to defend himself, and to the Chancellor's
questions he replied briefly, respectfully, and
quietly without any excuses or denials, save that

he solemnly protested that he had had no intelligence with Spain or any other foreign powers. He admitted signing the declaration that had brought Languedoc into the revolt and said that he was unwilling to make things better for himself by laying the blame on Monsieur. He attributed his conduct entirely to his own imprudence and ill fortune and refused to incriminate any of his friends. All this he said with the greatest calmness, showing only one brief moment of emotion when he did not reply to the question whether he had any children of his marriage, but covered his eyes with his hand.[1] To the Chancellor's final demand whether he recognized the gravity of his fault he replied that he deserved more than could be expressed.[2]

The whole proceedings lasted only about a quarter of an hour and then Montmorency was removed that the judges might consider their verdict and sentence. A few minutes later they interrupted their deliberations at the request of Montmorency, who had asked to be allowed to make a further statement. He now formally disculpated Guilleminet, the registrar of the Estates, the only witness against whom he had shown any bitterness, and

[1] Rénée, 146.

[2] Puységur (I, 133) relates that when Châteauneuf asked Montmorency his name, the Duke replied: "My name? Monsieur, you ought to know it. You ate my father's bread for long enough." Châteauneuf is supposed to have answered that such questions were no more than customary formalities. Although Desormeaux (439) and Monlaur (201) also quote this anecdote, it is probably apocryphal. At any rate it is not in consonance with the rest of the Duke's behaviour during his trial.

swore solemnly that he had compelled him to sign the declaration against his will.

In the circumstances the judges had no other alternative than to declare the prisoner guilty; the evidence was clear enough and he had made no attempt to defend himself, but had freely admitted his guilt. When they had expressed their opinions silently by uncovering themselves in the customary manner, sentence was pronounced to the effect that the Duc de Montmorency, premier peer and Marshal of France, Governor of the province of Languedoc, was to be degraded from all his honours, was to suffer the confiscation of all his property, and was condemned to be delivered into the hands of the executioner of high justice, who was to cut off his head on a scaffold erected in the Place de Salin. Although obliged to pass this sentence, nearly all the judges did so with the utmost reluctance, and many of them had been so affected by the nobility and gentleness of his bearing during the trial that as soon as they got out of the hall they made no attempt to conceal their grief.

Just as the Duke was about to leave the Parlement he complained of a pain in his heart and asked for a cup of wine to relieve his thirst. An usher brought one, but Launay, fearing that it might be poisoned, desired him to taste it himself first. This suspicion so annoyed the Duke that he

R

refused to drink, but got straight back into his carriage.

When he got back to the Hôtel de Ville, knowing that he would not be allowed to return to his room after he had heard his sentence read, he took off the suit of dark brown Spanish cloth he had worn at the trial and asked for the white suit he had had made at Lectoure. Turning to Arnoux he said to him with a smile: "'Father, we must enter all white into Paradise." Since he had had nothing to eat he was given some soup, which he found very bitter owing to the wounds in his throat. He recalled to mind the vinegar that had been given to the Saviour on the Cross and said: "God gives me this bitterness that I may remember the vinegar which Jesus Christ was given to drink and so may become entirely disgusted with life."

The King had sent for Launay, which had aroused in the hearts of the Duke's friends a faint ray of hope that it might be intended to pardon him at the last moment. In the meantime Montmorency conversed with the priest and thanked his guards and all who had administered to his comfort during his short imprisonment. All around him were weeping, both priests and soldiers, and the curious sight was seen of the intended victim himself endeavouring to console those who were to be left behind. He had become entirely reconciled to the thought of death and was satisfied that his sentence was just. "If I had listened," he said, "to the good advice of the Archbishop of Narbonne, the Comte de Rieux, and many others of my friends, God would never have abandoned me. I foresaw the storm, but I did not avoid it." He enquired of Father Arnoux whether God would allow souls in Paradise to look after those they had loved on earth, and when the priest replied that he believed so, cried joyously: "O my God, how many more consolations are you giving me than I have deserved!"

Charlus presently came from the King to demand from Montmorency his marshal's bâton and the cordon of the order of the Saint Esprit. The Duke handed them over to him, saying: "My dear friend and cousin, I willingly surrender the bâton and the order to my king, since he has decided that I am unworthy of his grace." Much affected by his interview with the Duke, Charlus returned to the King, whom he found playing chess with Liancourt and in a very ill humour, since wherever he looked he saw nothing but sorrowful and sullen faces.[1] The Duc de Châtillon had asked him to remark that the very looks, not only of all the courtiers, but also of all who came into the royal presence implored his clemency for the Duc de Montmorency. Charlus handed the

[1] Puységur, I, 134.

bâton and cordon to the King, and then falling on his knees at his feet he cried: "Ah, Sire, show mercy to Monsieur de Montmorency. His ancestors did so many great services to the kings who preceded you. Show mercy to him, sire." All those present also threw themselves on their knees and joined in Charlus's petition. But Louis XIII remained inexorable. "There can be no mercy, he must die," he said with cold finality.

Montmorency had never cherished any hope that he was to be reprieved and calmly proceeded with his preparations for death. In these last minutes a great humility had come upon him and he showed himself anxious to divest himself of anything that might savour of this world's vanity. After gazing steadfastly for some time at the crucifix he held in his hand he said: "Should I dare, criminal as I am, to go to death dressed with vanity, while I behold my innocent Saviour die naked on the Cross." He insisted upon removing his magnificent clothes and remained clad only in his shirt and drawers over which he threw a soldier's great-coat of coarse woollen material. He also cut off his long moustache and asked that it should be burnt.[1]

When Charlus and Launay had returned about noon Montmorency descended with them to the

---

[1] Tallémant des Réaux says that he also cut off his 'cadenette', the long lock of hair which was then worn hanging over the left shoulder, and that he sent both this and his moustache to his wife.

chapel of the Hôtel de Ville, followed by murmurs of grief and sympathy from all the bystanders. Two commissioners were already awaiting him in the chapel. Kneeling before the crucifix he heard his sentence read. He then rose and, addressing the commissioners in a firm voice, he said, "I thank you, messieurs. I beg of you to assure all your colleagues that I hold this decree of the King's justice as a decree of God's mercy." After this he fell again to praying, repeated his last act of contrition, and dedicated to God the sacrifice of his life. As a last favour he requested that the hour of his execution might be put forward from five to three o'clock so that he might meet his death at the same hour of the day as Jesus Christ had died. No difficulty was made in granting this request.[1]

Montmorency spent the interval before his execution seated on a bench by the balustrade of the Chapel in close converse with Father Arnoux. He assured the priest that he was convinced that by God's mercy this terrible blow would strengthen the soul and even the health of his beloved wife. As for himself, he had never felt stronger or more confident than he did now. "What is it that I feel in me, Father?" he asked, "I can assure you before God to whom I am about to answer that I have never gone to a ball, nor a banquet, nor a

[1] Pontis, 185.

battle with more satisfaction that I am going to
my death, and that if I did not by so many other
means know that there is a God, this feeling which
is fortifying me above Nature, so weak in itself,
would alone make me adore him. Promise me,
Father, that you will say nothing of this, for fear
that it might be attributed to some feeling of
vanity which is not there. I reveal it to you for
my consolation and your own, and to the honour
of God, who alone has brought all this to pass."

Almost at the last moment it had been decided
to alter the place of execution. It was to take
place, not in the Place de Salin before all the
people, but in the courtyard of the Hôtel de Ville
in the presence of the essential officials only.[1] The
change was represented as a last favour to Montmorency himself, but it is far more probable that
Richelieu decided upon it through fear that a
public execution might raise some display of popular feeling which might even culminate in an
attempt to rescue the Duke on the very scaffold.
Certainly the feeling of the townsfolk was wholly
in his favour and during the whole night before
the execution the churches had been thronged with
sorrowing worshippers.

With the utmost calm the Duc de Montmorency
proceeded to the scene of his death. The scaffold
had been erected at the entrance of the little

[1] The court was small and could not hold many spectators.

courtyard, which was now flooded with autumn sun-
light. The judges and the dignitaries of the town
in their red robes sat at the upper windows. The
Duke was saluted by all the guards as he passed
through their ranks to the scaffold, escorted by
Launay and attended by Arnoux and three other
Jesuit priests. As he caught sight of the statue of
Henri IV, for one moment his eyes became veiled
with tears. One of the priests asked if he wished
for anything. "No, Father," the Duke replied,
"I was looking at the statue of Henri IV. He was
a great and generous prince. I had the honour to
be his godson."[1]

The Duke had already cut off some of his hair,
but it was not yet short enough for the executioner's
purpose. Montmorency refused to permit his surgeon to supplant the headsman in the performance
of this office. "Let him do it," he said, "Jesus
Christ was not only crucified but attended by his
executioners." He himself helped the executioner
to uncover his neck and shoulders and held out
his bare arms to be bound. He had insisted that
all this should be done, although the King had
ordained as a favour to him that he need not be
bound and that the executioner was not to touch
him save for the fatal stroke itself. Montmorency
was determined to undergo all the humiliations
suffered by the Saviour. While he was being bound

[1] Desormeaux, 445; Rénée, 154.

he gave to Arnoux the crucifix he had hitherto held saying, "Take it, Father, the just must not be bound with the unjust."

After saluting with his accustomed grace all who surrounded him he mounted the scaffold with a firm step,[1] having first made a request to one of the priests who attended him to endeavour to prevent his head from falling off the scaffold on to the ground. It appears that he had always remembered as the most gruesome sight he had ever seen the spectacle of the head of an executed person rolling along the ground.

Without making any speech save a request to the priests to pray for him he knelt at once upon the scaffold, then, turning to the headsman, he said: "I forgive you willingly. Strike boldly!" Thereupon he laid his head on the block, but finding it too low and insecure he rose again and changed his position. The wound in his throat was agonizing him and he uttered a sharp exclamation of pain which caused the executioner to arrest his hand as it was about to descend. Montmorency called to him not to strike and once more adjusted his position. This time he stretched out his hands and called aloud: *"Domine Jesu, accipe spiritum meum."* The executioner's sword flashed down and

[1] According to tradition the scaffold was erected on a level with the first-floor windows (Rénée, 315).

severed the head from the body with one blow.[1]
As the Duke had hoped, his head fell near the
block and the executioner prevented it from falling
off the scaffold. It is said that the statue of Henri
IV was bespattered with the Duke's blood and
that the stains long remained visible.[2]

As soon as the execution was over the gates of
the courtyard were opened and the crowd rushed in.
The headsman held up the Duke's head aloft for
them to see, and then ensued an extraordinary
scene. The air was filled with exclamations of
woe and indignation. Men, women, and children
tore up fragments of the blood-stained pavement
to carry away with them as relics. Some even
drank the dead Duke's blood in the belief that
with it they might imbibe some of his courage.
For a like reason his very guards dipped their
swords in his blood.

In the evening Madame de Gramont with two
priests sent by Cardinal de la Valette arrived in
a carriage and bore away the body of the executed
Duke to the Abbey of St. Sernin.[3] When the
body was opened preparatory to embalming, and
the heart was removed to be given to the Jesuits

[1] Montmorency was executed not with an axe but with a slightly
curved scimitar which is still preserved at Toulouse. Puységur (I,
137) is in error in stating that the instrument employed was a species
of guillotine.

[2] Rénée, 315.

[3] Du Cros, 299; *Mercure*, 1632 XVIII, 843 (The latter account makes
no mention of Madame de Gramont, who was Claude de Montmorency,
daughter of Bouteville, wife of Antoine, Comte de Gramont, and mother
of Philibert, hero of the Gramont memoirs).

in fulfilment of a promise made by Montmorency, five balls were found in the corpse. The surgeons who conducted the autopsy were agreed that, though some of the wounds were serious, none of them would have proved mortal. After the head had been sewn on to the trunk again and the body had been embalmed it was placed in a leaden shell, and the doors of the chapel were opened to the people. Goulas relates that on the night of the execution, when the Duke's body was lying in the chapel, three ladies came in and remained there for three hours weeping and praying over the bier. When at last they rose to leave, one of them was so overcome that her companions had the greatest difficulty in leading her away.[1] He does not venture, however, to identify the mysterious lady. It cannot have been Marie Félice, who at this time was still unaware of her husband's death and, moreover, was far too ill to rise from her bed of sickness. Perhaps, then, it was one of the ladies who had loved him, or more probably still the Princesse de Condé, who had not been permitted to see her brother before his death.

For several days the people thronged the chapel eager to pay their last tribute to their former Governor, and finally the Duke's body was interred with great solemnity in the Chapel of St. Exupère, which since the days of Charlemagne

[1] Goulas, II, 207.

PLATE VIII

Marie Felice des Vrsins Duchesse de Montmorancÿ,
qui après la mort du Duc son Marÿ se retira dans
le Monastere de la Visitation de Moulins 3.e de
l'ordre, dont elle est Fondatrice, et ou elle est morte
Superieure le 5.e Juin 1666, agée de 66 ans.

P. Van-schuppen fecit

had received the earthly remains of saints and martyrs alone. For a whole month without interruption masses were said in the Chapel for the repose of the soul of Henri de Montmorency.

Montmorency's terrible death caused the utmost grief throughout the province where he had been adored. The whole of Languedoc went into mourning for him. When the tidings of his death were spread abroad, the shops in every town and village were shut. Those who approved of his death were few indeed and consisted only of his personal enemies. The rest of France was not even indifferent to his fate; the sternness of the King and the Cardinal was universally deprecated. By the people and the soldiery Montmorency had been adored, and to a man they openly lamented his death. Poets expressed their grief in verse; but few, if any, of the innumerable poems which were produced on this occasion possess any merit. The following, which appears to have appealed most to the public taste, will serve as a specimen.[1]

> The Mars of *France* is dead, we see
>   Great *Montmorency* is no more;
> Nor was the Hero Thunder free,
>   Although he Groves of Laurel wore.

[1] The English translation quoted above is to be found in a little book, *Observations upon the Government of the Kingdom of France, etc.* published in 1689. The English version is no worse than the original French which is printed in *Mercure François*, 1632, XVIII, 844–5.

Whilst all Mankind his Fortune grieves,
  That his untimely Race is run;
He only in our Verses lives,
  And by what his Sword has done.
Reader, if thou fain wou'dst know
  How he received this dire disgrace;
Behind him came the fatal blow,
  Death durst not look him in the Face.

At Court another feeling besides that of pity for
Montmorency himself added to the general consternation, for the nobility rightly regarded his
end as an overwhelming blow struck at their whole
class by the Cardinal. He had created a precedent
which they feared might be followed in their own
case. It must be admitted that there is much to
be said for Richelieu's action in adopting this
drastic means of suppressing rebellion. One of
France's sorest needs was peace within her own
borders, and this could never be attained while
there still existed a semi-independent, turbulent,
and rebellious nobility. Peaceful measures would
never suppress them; some sort of deterrent action
was needed, and the dread example of Montmorency's fate contributed more than anything else
to placing the nobility in their due position beneath
instead of alongside the Crown. Cardinal Richelieu
declared that, of all the nobles, Montmorency was
the one most dangerous to the Crown. "He was

the first peer of the realm, but of the humour of
those who have lived these last hundred years,
who have applied to their own aggrandisement
and their own interests the devotion which their
predecessors gave to their kings and to the state,
and of the humour of his father, who, in order to
make himself powerful in Languedoc, raised heresy
there and divided and weakened the King's
authority."[1]

The tragedy is that in all his treatment of
Montmorency Richelieu had from one point of
view been right all along. He was right in urging
the execution of Bouteville in the face of Montmorency's appeals; he was right in effecting the
abolition of the office of Grand Admiral; he was
right in attempting to sweep away the anomalous
jurisdictions in Languedoc; and he was right in
visiting Montmorency's rebellion with swift and
condign punishment. But, on the other hand, it
would be difficult, if not impossible, to absolve
the Cardinal of having been actuated all along
mainly by personal motives. Although he pleaded,
and pleaded with some justification, the interest
of the State, he was animated by pride, envy, and
hatred in his pursuit of Montmorency. Richelieu
was not impersonal. As minister he made no
scruple of disregarding the personal obligations
which as a man he owed to Montmorency; but the

[1] Richelieu, *Mémoires* (Mich et Pouj) VIII, 399.

man would not allow the minister to take into account the Duke's signal services to the State. In the whole course of the matter he acted vindictively, with ingratitude, and, worst of all, with hypocrisy. 'The Cardinal de Richelieu played his part marvellously in this,' says Goulas, 'for he interceded for his enemy; he spoke, he wept, he praised—but his praises were his funeral oration.'[1]

Louis XIII's true feelings in the matter are much more difficult to discover. Throughout he had seemed cold, callous, and implacable; but it appears to have been generally believed that he would have pardoned Montmorency, had not the Cardinal been so determined on his death and exercised all his wiles to close the King's heart against him.[2] Many times afterwards Louis expressed his regret at having allowed the execution to take place, and on his deathbed he summoned Condé to him to reiterate his regret.[3]

As for Monsieur, this contemptible prince did for once at least frankly recognize his share of the responsibility for his friend's death. He wrote a long and angry letter to the King maintaining that he had been tricked into making his unconditional submission by unofficial but solemn assurances that Montmorency would be pardoned.[4] He had

[1] Goulas, I, 206.
[2] Desormeaux, 399.
[3] Aumale, III, 248.
[4] The letter was actually composed by his secretary, Leonard Goulas, cousin of the author of the memoirs (Goulas II, 207).

understood that though Montmorency could not
be given his life as a condition of peace, since then
it would have appeared that the King had been
forced to come to terms, it would be granted to
him as a royal act of grace. There is no doubt that
Monsieur had received some such promise by the
instrumentality of the Cardinal, who, of course,
had never intended that it should be redeemed.
Nevertheless, this does not alter the fact that he
ought not to have agreed to abandon Montmorency
on any terms whatsoever. The stain on his honour
was never forgotten. Tallemant des Réaux relates
a story which throws some light on the opinion of
the King's brother thereafter held by his con-
temporaries. The Duc de Montbazon[1] was once
attending a party given by Monsieur and had
modestly taken a place towards the back of a
raised stand. Perceiving him there, Gaston invited
him to come more to the front and held out his
hand to help him down, whereupon Montbazon
remarked to him: "I am the first of your friends
whom you have helped to *descend* from the scaffold."
On this one occasion of his betrayal of Montmorency
he does seem to have been ashamed of himself.
He informed the King that after Montmorency's
death he could not remain with honour in France
and once more betook himself to the Netherlands.

---

[1] Louis de Rohan, Prince de Guéménée, Duc de Montbazon, husband
of that Princesse de Guéménée beloved of Montmorency.

Two Capucin monks were sent forthwith to the Duchesse de Montmorency to break the news of her husband's death to her and to carry her his last letter. Ever since her arrival at La Grange she had been lying in bed weeping incessantly and almost paralysed with grief, so that no one dared to go and break the news to her. In the end the gloom and sorrow of her attendants, which they could not conceal, made her divine the truth. Even though she had expected it, the shock was so great that a blood-vessel broke internally and for a week she lay at the point of death. At last, however, as Montmorency had hoped, her faith came to her aid and she was able to find some consolation in her religion. Her new spirit was shown by her cry: "O God, I loved no one but him, and you have taken him away that I may love no one but you."

EPILOGUE

Marie Félice at Moulins—Her inability to forgive the Cardinal—Her dignified answer to his compliments—Montmorency's body removed from Toulouse—The coffin escorted by Soudeilles—Its arrival at Moulins—Marie Félice builds a mausoleum—The Duke's tomb—Its inscription—The Duchess renounces the world—She is visited by Mademoiselle de Montpensier—She becomes Mother Superior of the convent—Her death.

For years after the tragedy Marie Félice lived in strict retirement in a house next to the Convent of the Visitation at Moulins. She never seemed to recover from the grief of her loss, although, as time passed she certainly derived much consolation from her religion. She did all in her power to rehabilitate her husband's memory, and it was under her instructions that Simon Du Cros wrote a life of the Duke in which his military exploits were related and the magnitude of his services to France extolled.

She attributed her husband's death to the Cardinal, and in spite of her gentle spirit she could never bring herself to forgive him until he too was dead. She herself told Mademoiselle de Montpensier that she had incessantly prayed God to vouchsafe her the charity to forgive him, but that it was long before she could bring herself to do so.[1]

In 1642, when the Court happened to be passing through Moulins, Richelieu had the temerity to send to offer her his compliments. Her answer was truly dignified. "Monsieur," she said to the Cardinal's gentleman, "inform your master that I am obliged to him for the honour he does me; but tell him also that my tears are not yet dry."[2]

Marie Félice's dearest wish was to provide a worthy resting-place for her husband's remains, and her first intention was to build a new Convent of the Visitation in Toulouse and to erect Montmorency's tomb in the chapel. But she was dissuaded from this course by the heads of the Order themselves, who were afraid that if other convents were built the Order would become too diffused and therefore disunited. The Duchess then determined to endeavour to have Montmorency's body brought to Moulins. The Regent, Anne of Austria, readily gave her consent, and the Duke's surviving sisters, the Princesse de Condé and the Duchesse de Ventadour, also approved the project. Condé at first offered some officious objections, but event-

---

[1] Montpensier, III, 350.

[2] Pitaval, 277.   Tallemant des Réaux relates the curious story that the Duchess had become very much bent through an internal inflammation, but that she wept so much for her husband that the inflammation dispersed through the eyes and she became as upright as before.

ually withdrew them.[1] Marie Félice had more
difficulty with the Chapter of St. Sernin, which,
supported by the Archbishop of Toulouse, expressed
itself unwilling to forgo the honour of having Montmorency buried in its chapel. It required a special
order from the Regent to wring a reluctant consent
from the Abbey.

In March, 1645, the leaden casket containing the
Duke's body was opened in order to prove the
identity of the corpse prior to its removal. So
well had the embalmers done their work that those
who witnessed the opening of the coffin afterwards
declared that it was almost impossible to credit
that the Duke's death had taken place as many as
twelve years ago.

The Duchess sent her faithful squire, Maurens,
to superintend the removal, and the honour of
conducting the corpse to Moulins was entrusted
at his own request to Soudeilles, Montmorency's
former Captain of the Guards, who since the tragedy
had been living in retirement on his own estates.[2]
Although he had always been opposed to the rebellion and had advised Montmorency against it,
as the Duke himself had admitted when, on his
return to the Hôtel de Ville after his trial, he
remarked that if he had followed the advice of
Soudeilles this misfortune would never have come
upon him,[3] Soudeilles had remained steadfast in

[1] Cotolendi, 204.   [2] Ibid, 205.   [3] Mercure, 1632, XVIII, 839.

his loyalty to his master and had firmly refused all offers of advancement made to him by Richelieu, who was ever anxious to secure for himself the services of men of his character and worth. He would never consent, he said, to serve under any other master.[1]

It was on Soudeilles' carriage, covered with a black velvet pall embroidered with silver and adorned with escutcheons bearing the arms of Montmorency, that the coffin was placed. The funeral car was drawn from Toulouse to Moulins by eight horses each led by a groom, and a large company of mourners followed behind. The Court had stipulated that all demonstrations were to be avoided, especially in Languedoc, and in consequence all large towns were traversed by night, the halts by day being made in small villages. But when the funeral procession reached Soudeilles' estate in the Limousin, in spite of the strict orders to the contrary all the nobility of the neighbourhood came out to meet it and a solemn service of commemoration was held in the church at Darnoy.[2]

On the evening of the 16th of March the coffin arrived at the convent at Moulins. The chapel was entirely hung with black and the Duchess was waiting in her accustomed place in the choir to see her husband's remains brought in. With a great effort she succeeded in restraining her grief

[1] Desormeaux, 380.   [2] Cotolendi, 108.

and only a few tears betrayed the intensity of her emotion. She requested that she might be left alone to watch over the corpse during this first night. In the course of the next few days countless masses for the repose of Montmorency's soul were said in all the churches in Moulins.[1]

For several years the Duke's body was temporarily interred in the existing chapel of the convent of Moulins while a new church was being built. The foundation stone was laid in 1648 and four years later the new mausoleum was completed and ready to house the magnificent tomb which was being made by the sculptor Augier, the designer of the famous Porte St. Denis at Paris.

The tomb, which took five years in the making, consisted of a white marble statue of the Duke lying upon a cushion, his right hand on his helmet, his left grasping the hilt of his sword. This was set upon a block of black marble four feet in height. A little behind the figure of the Duke was a white marble statue of Grief. Without consulting the Duchess, Augier had taken it upon himself to make this figure resemble her, and the likeness is said to have been striking. At either end of the tomb were seated statues a little larger than life representing Hercules and Liberality. Above again were figures of Religion and Nobility contained in niches in the wall. Between them was an urn

[1] Cotolendi, 109.

suspended from a cord which was being attached on either side by cherubs. Over all two angels held aloft the arms of Montmorency. Magnificent though she admitted it to be, the Duchess had several faults to find with the tomb. Through some mistake in the instructions given to the sculptor the Duke's face was turned away from instead of towards the altar. She was also extremely distressed that Augier had cut the figure of Grief in her likeness and endeavoured to persuade him to modify the resemblance, but was told that it was too late to do so. She did, however, succeed in getting him to cover the pristine nudity of the attendant cherubs.[1]

The inscription on the tomb read as follows:

HENRICO + II + MOMMORENCIACI + DUCUM +
ULTIMO + ET + MAXIMO
FRANCIAE + PARI + THALLASSIARCHO + POLEMARCHO +
TERRORI + HOSTIUM + AMORI + SUORUM

MARIA + FELIX + URSINA + EX + ROMANA +
STIRPE + CONJUX + UNICA
CUI + EX + IMMENSIS + VIRI + DIVITIIS + UNAE +
AMOR + VIVENTIS + ET + DEFUNCTI + CINERES

POST + EXACTOS + IN + CONJUGIO + FELI-
CISSIMO + ANNOS + XVIII +
MARITO + INCOMPARABILI + DE + QUO + DOLORE+
NIHIL + UNQUAM + POTUIT + NISI + MORTEM

BENEMERENTI + F.   AN   SAL.   ƆICIƆC.LII
SUI LUCTUS XX +

[1] Cotolendi, 247.

To Henri II, last and greatest of the Dukes of
Montmorency, peer of France, Admiral, Marshal,
dreaded by his foes, beloved by his friends; Marie
Félice des Ursins, of Roman race, his only consort,
who, of her husband's immense riches, cared only
for his love when living and his ashes when dead;
after eighteen years passed in the happiest of
unions; to the incomparable husband, from whom
she received no sorrow save his death; as a token
of her gratitude erected this monument in this
year of grace 1652, the twentieth of her grief.

Although the new chapel was finished in 1652
it was not until three years later that the
tomb was completed and set in place and the
Duke's remains were solemnly transferred to it.
Now at last Marie Félice had accomplished
her greatest desire, which cannot be better
expressed than in her own words: "What a
joy it is to me that I have been able to house
beneath the same roof my God and the husband
He gave me."

Two years later she finally renounced the world
and took the veil, as she had long wished to do.
Mademoiselle de Montpensier gives an account in
her memoirs of a visit she paid her when she was
with the Queen at Moulins in 1659.[1] Because she was
the daughter of Gaston d' Orléans she had hesitated
for a long time before going to see Montmorency's

---

[1] Montpensier, III, 349–351.

widow, but Marie Félice speedily assured her
that she need not have felt any embarrassment
on that score, since her father himself had always
visited her when he was passing through Moulins.
Mademoiselle gained the impression that the
Duchesse de Montmorency had never recovered
from the tragedy and that it still overshadowed
her whole life. "No one," she wrote, "has ever
had so true a grief nor has kept it up for so long,
for she is not yet recovered from it." The Duchesse
talked much and freely about her husband and
assured Mademoiselle that no passion had ever
been as great as that which she had had for him
and that she herself had sometimes had scruples
about it on the score of religion. Mademoiselle
described Marie Félice as being much enfeebled
by her grief, but thought that she must have
been very charming in her youth, though the
Queen had assured her that she had never been
beautiful.

In 1665 the Duchess, whose gentleness and
piety had won for her the love and veneration
of the nuns of the Convent of the Visitation, after
repeated refusals, at last consented to become their
Mother Superior. She did not long survive her
appointment, but died on June the 5th, 1666,
esteemed as a saint by all who had been fortunate
enough to know her in the days of her convent-
life. This was her true vocation. Though she had

given her heart to Montmorency, loving him with
a passion conceivably beyond the compass of most
women, she was of a temperament too gentle and
timid to be mated with a man to whom the hazards
of war were the very breath of life.

APPENDIX I

The sentence of the Parlement of Toulouse con-
demning the Duc de Montmorency to death had also
ordered the confiscation of all his goods and had re-
united the duchy of Montmorency to the Crown. But
Louis XIII treated the Duke's relatives with the
utmost generosity. On condition that they settled
Montmorency's debts and undertook to continue the
payment of the amounts due under their respective
marriage-settlements to the Duchesse de Montmorency
and the Constable's widow, he divided Montmorency's
property and estates among his three sisters and his
nephew, the Comte d'Alais,[1] with the exception of
the Château of Chantilly, which he kept for himself
as a hunting-box, though without the intention of
annexing it permanently.[2] On his death it returned
to the Montmorency estate, and the Prince de Condé
bought out the interests of his sisters-in-law.[3] The
Duchesse de Montmorency appears to have resigned
all her interest in her husband's property to his family
and to have retained only her personal fortune, which,
however, was considerable.[4]

In 1633 Louis XIII again erected the domain of

[1] Richelieu, *Mémoires* (Mich et Pouj) VIII, 419; *Lettres de don
des biens de feu Monsieur de Montmorency; Mercure,* 1632, XVIII,
978.
[2] Aumale, III, 250   [3] Clinchamp, *Chantilly,* 29
[4] Montpensier, III, 350

Montmorency into a duchy in favour of the Prince de Condé and his wife, Charlotte de Montmorency, sister of the last duke. The Condés thereupon assumed the title of Duc and Duchesse de Montmorency in addition to their numerous other titles. In 1689, by a readjustment of titles, the dukedom of Montmorency once again came into the possession of a descendant in the male line of that illustrious house. At the request of François Henri de Montmorency, Duc de Piney, a representative of a younger branch of the ancient family, Louis XIV transferred the title of Montmorency to the duchy of Beaufort, which Piney had purchased from the Duc de Vendôme. At the same time the name of the Condé duchy was changed to Enghien.

APPENDIX II

BIBLIOGRAPHY

The longest and most detailed accounts of Montmorency's career are to be found in:—

DU CROS. Simon Du Cros, *Histoire de la Vie de Henry Dernier Duc de Montmorency*, 1643

DESORMEAUX. J. L. Ripault-Desormeaux, *Histoire de la Maison de Montmorenci*, 1764. Tome III

PITAVAL. Gayot de Pitaval, *Causes Célèbres et Intéressantes*, 1775. Tome XIV

The narrative of Du Cros deals chiefly with the military side of the Duke's career. He accompanied him on several of his campaigns and actually participated in many of the events he describes. But since the book was written by command of the Duchess and dedicated to her, Du Cros is tactfully reticent about the Duke's private life. His omissions are, however, amply supplied by Desormeaux, Pitaval, and the four biographies of the Duchess.

COTOLENDI. C. Cotolendi, *La Vie de Madame la Duchesse de Montmorency, Supérieure de la Visitation de Ste Marie de Moulins*, 1684

RÉNÉE. Amédée Rénée, *Madame de Montmorency*, 1858

BAILLON. Comte de Baillon, *Madame de Montmorency*, 1880

MONLAUR. M. L. Monlaur, *La Duchesse de Montmorency*, 1898

The work of Rénée and Baillon on the 17th century is so well-known and so highly esteemed that it is scarcely necessary to state that both these biographies are wholly reliable. Cotolendi and Monlaur are inclined to be prejudiced in favour of the Duchess; but Monlaur's book has a distinct value in that he had access to documents which were not available to his predecessors.[1]

A few facts, mostly in the first chapter, have been derived from

Du Chesne. *Histoire Généalogique de la Maison de Montmorency*, 1624

Other authorities of which considerable use has been made throughout the book, as will be seen from the multitude of references in the footnotes, are:—

Mercure. *Le Mercure François : ou Suite de l'Histoire de nostre temps, sous le règne du très-Chrestien Roy de France et de Navarre Louys XIII*

This periodical, of which twenty-five volumes were published at various dates between 1619 and 1648, is a contemporary source of incalculable value.

Aumale. Duc d'Aumale, *Histoire des Princes de Condé*, 1886

Richelieu. *Mémoires de Cardinal Richelieu*

The new edition edited by Jules Lair for the Société de l'Histoire de France has been used for events up to the year 1627, which is as far as it goes at present; references to subsequent events are from the next best edition, that in the Collection Michaud et Poujoulat.

Bassompierre. *Journal de Ma Vie ; Mémoires du Maréchal de Bassompierre*

Tallemant des Réaux. *Historiettes*, 1862 (Édition Monmerqué)

Next in importance comes a group of authorities only less quoted because they do not cover the whole ground of the book, but deal only with certain events or persons.

Aigrefeuille. D. C. d'Aigrefeuille, *Histoire de la Ville de Montpellier*, 1737

Clinchamp. Comtesse Berthe de Clinchamp, *Chantilly*, 1902

Cousin. V. Cousin, *Madame de Sablé*

Echard. Laurence Echard, *History of England*

Épernon. *The History of the Life of the Duke of Espernon. Englished by Charles Cotton Esq.*, 1670

---

[1] Léonce de Bellesrives' *Une famille de Héros, ou Histoire des Personnes qui ont illustré le nom de Montmorenci*, 1855 contains nothing that is not to be found in one or another of these authorities.

GOULAS. *Mémoires de Nicolas Goulas*

HERBERT. *Autobiography of Lord Herbert of Cherbury*

MAIRET. Jean Mairet, *La Sylvie, Tragi-Comédie-Pastorale*

MAIRET. Jean Mairet, *La Silvanire ou La Morte-Vive du Sr Mairet. Dediée à Madame la Duchesse de Montmorency. Autres œuvres Lyriques du Sieur Mairet,* 1631

MONTPENSIER. *Mémoires de Mademoiselle de Montpensier*

MOTTEVILLE. *Mémoires de Madame de Motteville*

ORLÉANS. *Mémoires de feu Mr le Duc D'Orléans,* 1685 (Attributed to Algay de Martignac)

PONTIS. *Memoirs of the Sieur de Pontis. Faithfully englished by Charles Cotton,* 1694
There is a French edition in the Collection Michaud et Poujoulat.

PUYSÉGUR. *Mémoires de Messire Jacques de Chastenet, Seigneur de Puységur,* 1690

STANLEY. Thomas Stanley, *Sylvia's Park by Théophile,* 1651

THÉOPHILE. Théophile de Viau, *Les Oeuvres du Sieur Théophile,* 1644

THÉOPHILE. Théophile de Viau, *La Maison de Sylvie,* 1624.
Stanley's *Sylvia's Park* is a translation of this work.

CONTEMPORARY PAMPHLETS.

L'Entrée de Madame de Montmaurensi a Montpelier, 1617. A facsimile reprint of this was published at Montpellier in 1873.

Récit véritable de la reprise de Chaumeras, 1628

Lettres de Monseigneur le Prince de Condé. Ensemble celle de Monseigneur de Montmorency, envoyée au Roy, sur le sujet du sieur de Bouteville, 1627

Mémoire donné a Mr D'Aiguebonne allant trouver Monsieur de la part du Roy, le 9 Septembre, 1632

Instruction du procez de Monsieur le Mareschal de Montmorency Duc et Pair de France, 1649

Lettres de don des biens de feu Monsieur de Montmorency, 1633. This was printed by royal command and contains other papers relating to the disposition of the Duke's estate.

The story of Montmorency's death and of the events which led up to it is based mainly on four contemporary accounts, which have all obviously been derived from the same source, but differ considerably in matters of detail and in the arrangement and extent of their contents.

I. *Histoire Véritable de ce qui s'est passé a Thoulouze a la fin du mois d'Octobre* 1632
    Printed in the series *Trésor des Pièces Toulousaines* in 1859 from a contemporary manuscript, the whereabouts of which is not stated.

II. *Relation de la fin qu'a faite M de Montmorency le 30 octobre a 2 heures après midi*
     A contemporary manuscript, No. 2359, in the Bibliothèque Mazarin. This has also been printed, in 1859.

III. *Histoire Véritable de tout ce qui s'est faict et passé dans la ville de Thoulouze, en la mort de Monsieur de Montmorancy*
      A pamphlet published in 1633.

IV. *Relation veritable de ce qui s'est passé au procez criminel de Monsieur de Montmorency, Pair et Marechal de france, condamné et executé a mort en la ville de Toulouze, le 30 jour d'octobre* 1632
     A manuscript in the author's possession. It is clearly written in a 17th century hand on one hundred and thirteen leaves roughly bound in contemporary marbled paper. A complete list of its contents follows.

Procez criminel de Messire Henry Duc de Montmorency, Pair et Maréchal de France, Gouverneur et Lieutenant général pour le Roy en la Provence de Languedoc, condamné et Executé a mort en la ville de Thoulouze, le trentième jour d'octobre 1632.
Extrait des Régistres de Parlement.
The depositions of the military witnesses taken at Narbonne in October.[1]
Interrogatory in Toulouse on October the 24th of Pierre Guilleminet, Registrar of the Estates of Languedoc.
The King's order for Montmorency's trial.
Two interrogatories of the Duc de Montmorency.
Resumptions et confrontemens du vingthuitième octobre, mil six cent trente-deux.
Dicts et conclusions du Procureur General du Roy.

[1] This and the other items described in English have no headings in the manuscript.

Réponses sur la scellette du trentième octobre mil six cent
trente deux.
Arrest de condamnation.
Lettres du Roy ordonnant l'execution du susd. Arret en
l'hotel de ville.
Lettre de Mosieur le Duc d'Orléans au Roy.
Lettre du dit Sr d'Angoulesme a Mr le Cardinal de Richelieu.
Relation véritable, de ce qui s'est fait et passe dans la ville
de Thoulouze, en la mort de Monsieur de Montmorency.
Included in this last section under a separate heading is:
Lettre de Monsieur le Duc de Montmorency a Madame sa
Femme.

For the general history of the period Lavisse et
Rambaud's *Les Guerres de Religion* (*Histoire Générale*,
Tome V) and the admirable sketch of Richelieu by Richard
Lodge in the Foreign Statesmen Series have been of great
service. The author has had recourse to various French
biographical dictionaries and *Nobiliaires*, with no very
satisfying result except, perhaps, that of increasing his
long-standing admiration for our own *Dictionary of
National Biography*.

T

INDEX

275